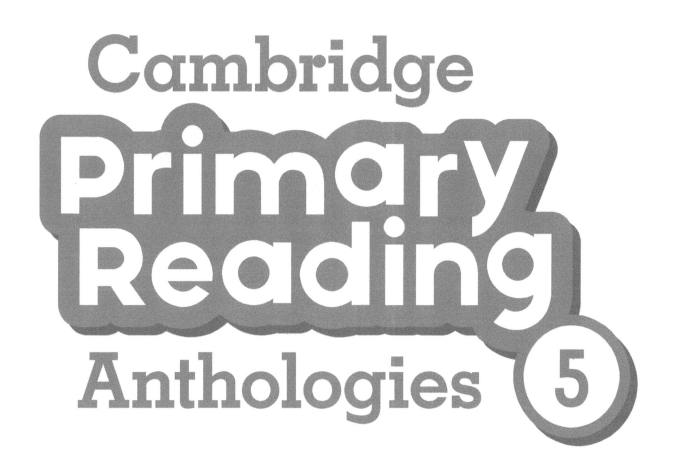

Cambridge Primary Reading Anthologies 5

T0372595

Student's Book
with Online Audio

CAMBRIDGE
UNIVERSITY PRESS

Scope and Sequence

Unit 1 How can we make a difference?

	Genre	Key Words	Reading Strategy
Fiction *Everybody's Park*	Realistic Fiction	gather, abandoned, lot, weeds, scatter, raise money, overhear, flyer, brainstorm, ideal	Asking Questions
Nonfiction *The Power to Change the World*	Magazine Profile of Environmental Activist	activist, protest, reduce, emissions, avoid, crisis, refugee, carbon footprint, severe, impact	Identifying Cause and Effect

Unit 2 How can we make our dreams come true?

	Genre	Key Words	Reading Strategy
Fiction *The Honorary First-Graders*	Realistic Fiction	anxious, routine, pluck, pail, assemble, shrink, teardrop, stunned, disrespectful, eager	Identifying Literary Elements
Nonfiction *A Dream That Changed a Nation*	Biography of Civil Rights Leader	separate, sunrise, debate, unfair, peaceful, victory, march, perseverance, inequality, balcony	Identifying Author's Purpose

Unit 3 How can we deal with natural disasters?

	Genre	Key Words	Reading Strategy
Fiction *A Quick Escape*	Science Fiction	humidity, glacier, extreme, adjust, drizzle, refreshing, bulky, drenched, stranded, turbulence	Visualizing
Nonfiction *The Top Five Natural Disasters in History*	Informational Text on Natural Science	powerful, erupt, bison, geyser, populated, tremor, record (v), fortunate, economic, unpredictable	Using Graphic Sources

Unit 4 What makes going to a show so exciting?

	Genre	Key Words	Reading Strategy
Fiction *The Twisted Tale of the Golden Goose*	Play	clown, comedian, enter, juggle, somersault, kingdom, exit, tall tale, hospitality, reign	Summarizing (fiction)
Nonfiction *When Actions Speak Louder Than Words*	Magazine Article on the Arts	expression, gesture, captivated, complicated, rely on, choreographed, represent, posture, attitude, pose	Summarizing (nonfiction)

Unit 5 How can we stay healthy?

	Genre	Key Words	Reading Strategy
Fiction *You Shouldn't Eat a Dozen Birthday Cakes* and *Jake, Who Only Ate Cake*	Poetry	dozen, munch, throat, burst, swear, shrug, beg, nibble, ache (v), blurred	Making Inferences
Nonfiction *Staying Healthy: Just Ask the Experts*	Health Advice Column	obesity, cholesterol, appetizing, boredom, cramp, abdomen, endurance, insomnia, expose, snore	Using Background Knowledge

Unit 6 Why is language special?

	Genre	Key Words	Reading Strategy
Fiction *Jaynie of the Daintree*	Realistic Fiction	capture, stationary, soar, circular, driftwood, mangrove, horizon, riverbank, ripple, fluorescent	Analyzing Plot
Nonfiction *Where in the World Does English Come From?*	Magazine Article on Social Studies	compose, integrate, inhabitant, variation, invade, settle, etymology, influence (v), derive, jumble	Identifying Fact and Opinion

Unit 7 How do machines help us?

	Genre	Key Words	Reading Strategy
Fiction *The Broken Well*	Historical Fiction	handlebars, lower (v), rusty, bracket, support (v), strain, scrape, flat tire, pedal, force	Making Connections
Nonfiction *Will Everything Be Automated?*	Pro/Con Discussion of Technology	automation, intricate, efficient, install, pedestrian, surgery, mechanical, assist, incision, precision	Identifying Main Idea and Supporting Details

Unit 8 How do we know what happened in the past?

	Genre	Key Words	Reading Strategy
Fiction *The Famous Detective Fox and the Museum Hall Mystery*	Mystery	attract, armor, spread out, arch, breeze, vent, notice (v), consider, silk, chopsticks	Evaluating
How History Changes	Informational Text on History	vivid, bury, snapshot, graffiti, prehistory, propose, gorge, nomadic, monolith, carve	Monitoring and Clarifying

Unit 9 Why does biodiversity matter?

	Genre	Key Words	Reading Strategy
Fiction *Rahui and the Sierra Tarahumara*	Realistic Fiction	rugged, remedy, ailment, herb, clearing, wary, peer (v), creep, spy, soothe	Understanding the Meaning of Words in Context
Nonfiction *The Secrets of the Tides*	Earth Sciences Report	shoreline, high tide, low tide, bay, bulge (v), align, intertidal zone, tide pool, seaweed, sea urchin	Paraphrasing

1 How can we make a difference?

Key Words

1  **Preview the Key Words.**
1.1

gather   abandoned   lot   weeds   scatter

raise money   overhear   flyer   brainstorm   ideal

2 **Read the definitions and write the Key Words.**

a to collect together _____

b left alone and not taken care of _____

c the best possible thing or situation _____

d to collect money for a cause _____

e to think of ideas in a group _____

f to drop or spread randomly _____

Pre-reading

3 📖 **Read the title and look at the pictures on pages 5–9. Write two questions you have about the text.**

a _____

b _____

4 🎧 **Listen and read.**
1.2

Everybody's Park

By Steph Kilen · Illustrated by Sheila Cabeza de Vaca

It was the big day: the day work was to begin on the new community park. Paola and James were getting work gloves while their parents gathered tools. The abandoned lot had been there for years, but it had gotten worse and worse. The weeds and grass had grown to their knees, and garbage was scattered all around. The nearby walls and fences had been spray-painted with graffiti. There was even an old tire and a ripped-up couch missing a cushion. Kids tried to play in the area, but their parents warned them against it because of all the broken glass on the ground. "But where else can we play?" James and Paola had asked.

One day, a few months ago, James and Paola were talking about where they could meet some friends. James's cousin had a small park in her neighborhood. "There's equipment for climbing and trees and benches. There's a wall that's like the chalkboard in our classroom for drawing on with chalk. We played there all afternoon. I wish we had a space like that," said James.

"Too bad all we have is that terrible lot," Paola said. "Wouldn't it be great if that was a park?"

James and Paola told James's mom their idea. "Cleaning it up would take some work, and we could do that," she said. "But the equipment would cost money."

The next day, James and Paola were hanging out at the playground, talking about how they might raise money to buy the equipment. Ben and Ahmed overheard them and were curious. "We want to build a park, but can't figure out how to raise the money," Paola said.

Ben suggested a lemonade stand. Ahmed said, "What about a car wash?"

Ada, who had been listening, interrupted. "We could gather all the toys and clothes we've grown out of and have a garage sale!"

Every weekend they tried one of the ideas. The first weekend the lemonade stand raised a little money, but not even enough to buy the wood for one bench. The next weekend they tried a bake sale and made a sign that said, "Help Build Our Park!" Ada and Ahmed were sure to tell everyone what the money from the sale was for. "Are you going to do another sale?" Mr. Barns asked.

"Next weekend we are having a garage sale," Ada said.

"Well," Mr. Barns said, "you should make some announcements to put up around town so more people know about it."

The next day, James and Paola made flyers with a photo of the lot and bright letters announcing the garage sale. Then, they put them up around the neighborhood. The kids got their parents to donate some items to the garage sale as well. They raised a lot of money, but they needed more. James's dad had an idea. He set up an online donation page so people could contribute that way as well.

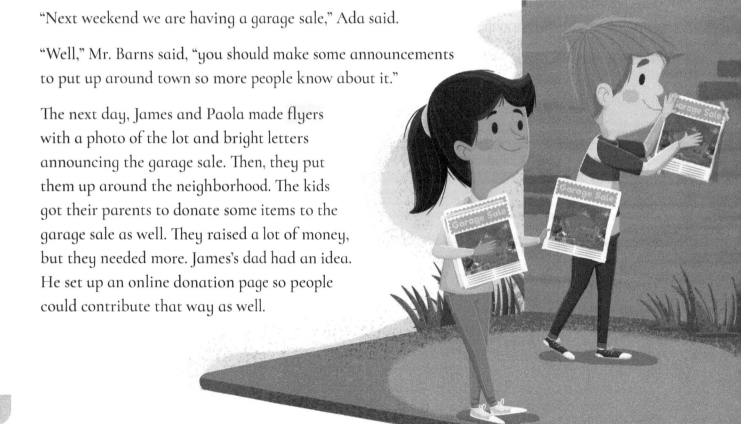

As word spread about what they were doing, they raised more and more money, and more and more people wanted to get involved. Some gave extra money. Some donated materials for the project. In a few months, their fundraising efforts had been successful, and they had enough money to begin their project. They knew they had to clean up the space, but then what would they do?

They organized a meeting to brainstorm ideas for making the park an ideal environment. They all agreed there should be some playground equipment, but there were some other great ideas, too! Ben liked to read more than climb. So, he suggested a weatherproof box where people could leave and take books. He also suggested a hammock for reading in. Ada thought it would be fun to put up some bird feeders and birdhouses. Ahmed thought the park would look nicer with some flowers. "And how about a vegetable garden?" Paola said. "Our parents are always telling us how important vegetables are," she said, and they all laughed but agreed it was a good idea. James suggested a chalkboard wall like the one at his cousin's park. "Maybe then there wouldn't be so much graffiti," he said.

They had the money and all the plans, so it was time to get started. At first it wasn't much fun. The kids helped pick up the trash and pull weeds and vines, while their parents moved the larger trash and cut down a rusted piece of fence. It was hard work, but by the end of the day, the lot looked much better. "There's still so much to do!" James said. The ground was hard, and grass grew in patches in some places, while other spots were full of stones.

The next workday, the kids moved stones and raked up the lot. Ahmed's mom came by with some snacks and juice and a big roll of paper. She spread it out on the ground and invited the kids to gather around it. They looked at the squares and circles with some confusion until Ahmed said, "It's the plan for the park!" His mom, who was a designer, had made plans for the space so they knew what went where and what they had to do. She pointed out where the equipment, trees, birdhouses, and chalkboard would go. She showed them where they needed to do some digging to plant grass and plants. Paola, James, and their parents handed out shovels, and everyone got to work. "Now, I can see it!" Ada said, and they all agreed.

For weeks they worked laying out the park. They built the benches, birdhouses, and boxes for plants. Then, they dug holes and shoveled dirt. Green Thumb Greenhouse donated grass, plants, and a few small trees. "How are we going to hang a hammock on those tiny trees?" Ben asked. "Just wait," Paola's mom said with a wink. And they all got to work planting. It seemed like all the work was done, but Ben's dad said they had one more week of work ahead of them. When they arrived at the site the next week, there were no tools or gloves, just some snacks. That's when the best part happened: the swings and climbing equipment arrived! The kids helped unload the trucks, and the parents set up the equipment.

When they were done, there was one more box in the truck, and Paola's mom asked Ben to get it. Ben and Ahmed opened it and found several colorful hammocks. "Where did these come from?" asked Ben. "Mrs. Parson donated these. She brought them from Mexico!" Paola's mom replied. "But where can we hang these?" Ahmed asked. "Look!" James's dad said, and pointed to several hooks on the equipment, fence, and nearby wall. Ahmed's mom had designed it so the hammocks could be moved around. The kids grabbed the hammocks and raced to hang them in different spots.

Throughout all the work, Ada's dad had been digging a shallow path through the space. While the kids swung in their hammocks, admiring all they had done, Paola's dad pulled up in his company's cement truck, and Ada's mom pulled up in their van. "What's that for?" James asked, pointing to the cement truck. "Ada!" Paola said. "We're making a path so Ada can use the park, too!" The door on the van opened, and Ada came out on a special ramp for her wheelchair. All the friends rushed to greet her.

"This is so cool!" she exclaimed. "I wish I could have helped."

"You can!" said Paola. "Next weekend we are going to paint the benches and birdhouses."

The next week, the neighbors had a big party in the park. Everyone clapped when they raised the sign that said "Everybody's Park." The kids, with splotches of paint on their arms and cheeks, read the names of everyone who contributed and revealed a sign with their names. It seemed like everything was done, but the kids had one more idea! They invited everyone to join them there the following weekend for an art project. James said, "We're going to paint garbage cans to look like animals and monsters to help keep the park clean!"

Key Words

1 **Use the Key Words to solve the riddles.**

a Wild plants growing free.
They're everywhere to see.

_____

d Sisters are talking to one another.
You catch a few words about
their brother.

_____

b Hand it out or send by mail
So they'll fly to your sale.

_____

e You can lend us a hand!
Clean this empty piece of land.

_____

c More ideas we can form
When we all try to

_____.

f Many peanuts we

_____

so the squirrels and birds will
get fatter.

Comprehension

2 **Answer the questions.**

a Why did the children need to raise money? _____

b Who designed the plan for the park? _____

c When did the children have the bake sale? _____

d Where did the small trees come from? _____

e How did the children hang up the hammocks? _____

f What did they paint on the garbage cans? _____

3 🖥 **Look at the questions you wrote in Activity 3 on page 4. Which ones were answered in the story? Write the answers.**

_____

_____

4 **Write two new questions that are answered in the text. Use who, what, when, where, why, or how.**

a _____?

b _____?

Digging Deeper

5 Complete the graphic organizer by matching the people to their contributions.

| Mr. Barns | Paola's dad | Mrs. Parson | Green Thumb Greenhouse |
| Ben and Paola | Ahmed's mom | Ada's dad | |

Donated Items	Donated Expertise	Donated Work
_____	_____	_____
_____	_____	_____
_____		

6 Write four other ways different people contributed to the park.

a _____

b _____

c _____

d _____

7 Do you think "Everybody's Park" is a good name? Why or why not?

_____

Personalization

8 Circle problems in your local community.

abandoned animals

no places for kids to play

no green spaces

litter

graffiti

9 Decide which problem you want to solve or propose a different problem in your local community. Answer the questions.

a Who would you involve to help you?

_____

b What would you do?

_____

c How would you raise money for the project?

_____

d What would you call your project?

_____

How can we make a difference?

Key Words

1 **Preview the Key Words.**
1.3

activist

protest

reduce

emissions

avoid

crisis

refugee

carbon footprint

severe

impact

2 **Match.**

activist

crisis

carbon footprint

reduce

severe

avoid

noun

verb

adjective

to try to not do something

very bad or harmful

to make smaller

a dangerous situation

a person who calls for strong action or change

the amount of greenhouse gas a person puts into the environment

Pre-reading

3 **Look at pages 13–15 and read the captions. Answer the questions and complete the sentences.**

a Who is the text about? _____

b Her goal is _____

c The text wants to **inform** / **entertain**.

d Two problems the text tells us about are _____

4 **Listen and read.**
1.4

The Power to Change the World

By S.B. Harris

Can just one person make a difference?
Greta Thunberg
Born: 2003, Sweden
Occupation: Student, Climate Activist

In many ways, Greta Thunberg is like any other teenager. She has two pet dogs, and she likes to eat noodles. In other ways, she is less typical. Greta is an activist, and she is famous. She also has attention deficit hyperactivity disorder (ADHD) and autism. Greta has a unique way of seeing things, and that helps her focus on making a difference in the world.

Greta began a protest in August 2018. That summer, Sweden experienced the country's hottest temperatures in hundreds of years. Greta became so worried that she went on strike. She didn't attend school for three weeks. Instead, she sat alone outside Sweden's parliament building and held up a large sign that said, "School Strike for Climate" in Swedish. She wanted the Swedish government to reduce carbon emissions, a type of air pollution that causes global warming. (In case you're wondering, Greta wasn't just lazy or trying to avoid school. She did all her schoolwork on the street!)

Then, people shared Greta's message on the Internet. Soon, many more people joined her protest. Greta's strike was so successful that it turned into an international movement called Fridays for Future. By September 20, 2019, more than four million people in 170 countries joined Greta in the Global Climate Strike!

School Strike for Climate

What Is Greta's Message?

Greta wants everyone to know that there's a climate crisis. We can't avoid dealing with it any longer. And, we must all take action right now. She wants people to use only clean energy and stop using fossil fuels like coal, oil, and natural gas. Using fossil fuels releases harmful gases into the atmosphere.

Why is that her message? Because Greta is very concerned about the negative effects of climate change. They can include fires, droughts, food shortages, flooding, and other problems. All of these problems are bad enough, but they can also force some people to become climate refugees. Climate refugees have to leave their homes because of the environmental problems in their country or region. Greta understands how difficult it is for these people. And she wants everyone to know that climate change is a serious problem around the world.

Greta traveled to the United States on the Malizia II, an environmentally friendly sailboat.

Greta has made a lot of changes in her own life to reduce her carbon footprint. She doesn't eat meat, and she doesn't travel by plane. That's why she travels around Europe by train and went to North America on a special type of sailboat. The boat, the *Malizia II*, runs on clean energy. It uses wind power and electricity from solar panels and hydroelectric generators. It doesn't put any carbon dioxide into the environment. And, in October 2019, she traveled by electric car in Canada partly to protest Canada's oil industry.

Greta's goal isn't to become famous. It's to change the world.

Why Should People Listen to Greta?

We don't all need to change our lives in the same ways that Greta has. But we do need to listen to her message and start making changes to the way we live. Some people think that conservation and recycling are enough to save the environment. Greta is convinced that they are no longer enough. She thinks we need to change society. If humans don't stop using fossil fuels, climate change will get worse. There will be more severe weather, like droughts, flooding, and hurricanes.

Greta says, "Activism works. So act."

Even a small temperature increase will lead to bigger wildfires.

There won't be enough water in some places, and then it will be harder to grow food. Many plants and animals will die. Life on Earth will change. Soon, there may be no coral reefs because ocean temperatures will rise even more. Endangered animals, such as elephants, orangutans, and polar bears, may disappear. Someday, glaciers and polar ice caps will melt. Then, oceans will rise and some cities will be underwater. As Greta has said, "You must take action. You must do the impossible. Because giving up can never be an option."

Coral reefs, like the Great Barrier Reef, are dying because of global warming.

Greta has spoken in front of many international organizations, including the U.K. Parliament, the European Union Parliament, the World Economic Forum, and the United Nations. She has asked world leaders to change the way things work. She was even nominated for a Nobel Peace Prize. And, in September 2019, she became the youngest person ever awarded the "alternative" Nobel Peace Prize, or Right Livelihood Award. In just one year, Greta has inspired many others to demand climate action in their own countries. She has had a huge impact all over the world!

The impact of climate change is more severe in polar regions.

Key Words

1 **Complete the sentences.**

| refugees | protest | reduce | avoid | impact | emissions |

a Some governments want to _____ dealing with the problem of climate change.

b Fossil fuels have a negative _____, or effect, on the environment.

c Some people became climate _____ after Hurricane Maria.

d A special test checks the _____ your car releases into the atmosphere.

e My brother participated in a _____ against climate change.

f We all need to _____ the amount of garbage we produce.

Comprehension

2 **Read and circle *T* (true) or *F* (false).**

a More than four million people in 170 countries participated in Fridays For Future.   T   F

b Greta traveled across Canada by electric car.   T   F

c Greta Thunberg went on strike after Sweden's coldest summer.   T   F

d Greta flew to New York City.   T   F

e Greta won a special Nobel Peace Prize.   T   F

3 **Circle the correct options. (There may be more than one.)**

1 What is Greta's main goal?

  a to become famous

  b to win a Nobel Peace Prize

  c to change the world

2 How has Greta attracted attention to her cause according to the article?

  a She wrote a school essay on climate change.

  b She spoke in front of international organizations.

  c She became a climate refugee.

3 What are some possible effects of climate change?

  a There will be more droughts and wildfires.

  b The polar regions will get colder.

  c Coral reefs will die.

  d It will be easier to grow food.

  e There will be more endangered animals.

Digging Deeper

4 📧 **Read the causes and write the effects.**

a People shared Greta's message on the Internet.

_____

_____

b People experience environmental problems where they live.

_____

_____

c Ocean temperatures rise even more.

_____

_____

d There isn't enough water in some places.

_____

_____

5 **Answer the questions.**

a Why does Greta have a unique way of seeing things?

_____

b What modes of transportation does she use? Why?

_____

c Why doesn't Greta eat meat?

_____

d Why doesn't Greta think recycling and conservation are enough?

_____

e Has Greta been successful? Why or why not?

_____

_____

Personalization

6 **Write five things YOU can do to fight climate change.**

a _____

b _____

c _____

d _____

e _____

2 How can we make our dreams come true?

Key Words

1 **Preview the Key Words.**
2.1

anxious   routine   pluck   pail   assemble

shrink   teardrop   stunned   disrespectful   eager

2 **Match the Key Words to the words with the same meaning.**

1 anxious	a excited
2 pail	b gather together
3 assemble	c rude
4 stunned	d bucket
5 disrespectful	e nervous
6 eager	f surprised
7 shrink	g pick
8 pluck	h reduce in size

Pre-reading

3 **Look at the pictures on pages 19–23 and make predictions.**

a Where does the story take place? _____

b Who are the main characters? _____

c How are the characters related to each other? _____

4 **Listen and read.**
2.2

The Honorary
First-Graders
Inspired by a True Story

By Sarah Steinberg • Illustrated by Emmanuel Urueta

"Wake up, Soo-Jin." It's still dark out when I sit up in bed and rub my eyes. Grandmother is standing over my bed. She hands me a cup of steaming tea, and I start to feel anxious again before I can remember why.

"Soo-Jin, do you know what today is?" Grandmother asks. This is not her usual routine. Grandmother only wakes me up before dawn one day of the year. On all the others, my alarm goes off, and I meet her in the kitchen for breakfast, where she asks me about my day ahead: "Have you done your homework? Are you ready for the spelling test? Have you memorized the math formulas?"

But today is different, and I look forward to this day every year because it is the first day of the strawberry harvest. All those juicy, red strawberries just waiting to be plucked from the plants and put into my pail. The harvest is usually my favorite time of year, but today I'm not so excited. I remember the terrible news we got yesterday, when our school principal assembled all eight of us in his office.

Principal Park looked very serious as we stood around him. "Children," he said, "I have some bad news." Gi-Nam and Nara, the only two kindergarteners in our school, began to cry. Not me. I'm twelve, and I'm pretty tough. Principal Park continued, "When our small town was bigger, there were many children who lived here. We built this school for them, but our town has shrunk and so has our student population. Ten years ago the school had 25 students. Now, it's just the eight of you, and we don't have enough students to keep the school open."

"What will happen to us?" asked Shanae, my best friend in the village. She sounded as if she might cry, too.

"The school will close down, and you will have to go elsewhere," Principal Park said. "Some of you will move to bigger cities where you have relatives. I wish I could help, but we can't continue to operate the school when we have so few students here. I'm sorry."

I couldn't believe what I was hearing, but I understood that you can't have a school without enough children.

That was yesterday. Today, our strawberries need to be harvested. The air is cool as we pick the berries. While Grandmother hums contentedly, I drop my strawberries into my pail. My heart is heavy. I should be happy, but I'm not. The fruits, in the shape of teardrops, make me want to cry. I guess I'm not so tough after all.

"What's the matter?" Grandmother asks.

"Principal Park gave us bad news yesterday," I say.

Grandmother stops humming. "What did he say?" she asks.

"He said our school will shut down because there aren't enough students. What will I do?"

Grandmother stops picking now, too, and her face, normally cheerful, changes. The sides of her mouth turn down, and her eyes go cold. I know that look; she always gets it when she's thinking hard.

"When I was even younger than you, I had to quit school," she tells me. "I was one of the smartest students in my class, but I had not yet learned to read. Like you, my mother lived in another city for work. But then she got sick, and I had to find work and help my family. Soo-Jin, I'm ashamed to tell you that I never learned to read."

I cannot imagine my grandmother not being able to do anything. At seventy-two years old, she is the smartest person I know and the one who can persevere through anything. She knows how to make a little money go so far that I hardly ever notice that we are poor.

"You? You can't read?" I ask, stunned. My grandmother shakes her head sadly.

"I can recognize a few words, but it was always my ambition to learn. So, Soo-Jin, we will not let that happen to you because you are too smart and creative. You will have a career! You must go live with your Auntie Pearl," my grandmother says firmly. My Auntie Pearl never had children, and she lives in Busan, a big city that is a long drive away. Then, my grandmother says, a little more gently: "Wouldn't that be a good adventure?"

I try to imagine leaving everything that I know. I picture myself in my Auntie's apartment in Busan, in the middle of a loud and busy city, and all of the things I know and love—my room, my friends, my grandmother's soup, my grandmother—far away.

"No!" I say, full of emotion. "I don't want to go. I want to stay here with you!"

I drop my pail and run away across the field, and I keep running, right across town, past the temple and through the forest. I end up at Dasan Chodang, the little house where the great Korean scholar Jeong Yakyong once wrote many important books. It's a tourist site now, but people don't visit it much anymore. Just like the man who wrote his books here, I come here when I need to think. I sit on the floor and try to calm down, and that's when I have my idea.

I start walking to Shanae's house. She lives with her brother, her parents, and her grandmother, and that's who I want to speak to. I get to her house and ring the bell, and her grandmother greets me at the door with a smile. I bow politely, and she invites me in.

"Thank you, but I only came here to ask you a question. I don't want to be disrespectful," I say. Shanae's grandmother nods at me, so I continue. "Did you go to school? Did you learn to read?" I ask.

Shanae's grandmother laughs. "I went to school," she says, "but I stopped when I was still very young. We had a bad harvest at the farm, and my parents needed me at home. I can read a few words and write my name," she says, "but I can't read or write very well. I would like to learn, though, because I want to read books aloud to my grandchildren."

I had found two grandmothers, and I knew I could find more.

Now it's two days later. We must look like a strange group with me leading the way, and a gang of elderly grandmothers following behind me. In the principal's office, I make formal introductions to Principal Park, even though he already knows all of the women.

Then, I say, "I know our school registration is low, but what if we could register these eight grandmothers today?"

Principal Park looks over at our town's grandmothers. What does he see? A group of grandmothers with gray hair and tired faces? Or does he see a group of eager students, hopeful and ready to go back to school? I hold my breath.

My grandmother steps forward and says, "Principal Park, it has been my dream to learn to read and write since I was a young child. I want to enroll in school now. Even if I'm an old lady, I can still be a student."

Principal Park grins. "If you are half as smart as your granddaughter, I'm sure you will do just fine," he says.

And now? Here we are. Every day the school bus takes us all to school, our honorary first-graders sitting at the back of the bus, smiling and laughing with their notebooks in their hands.

So that is how I doubled attendance at my school and saved it from closing, and how my grandmother and her friends began elementary school again. And, you know, there's some advantage to going to school with your grandmother. For instance, she always keeps a hard candy in her pocket so that she can give it to me during recess.

Key Words

1 **Complete the crossword puzzle.**

Across
1 worried about what might happen
2 the shape of a falling drop of water
6 a round container with a handle

Down
1 to come together in a group
3 a regular way of doing something
4 to pick something, like a berry
5 excited and ready for something

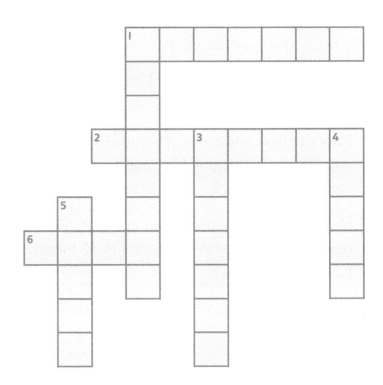

Comprehension

2 **Read and circle Y (yes), N (no), or DS (doesn't say).**

a Soo-Jin's grandmother always wakes her up before it gets light.   Y   N   DS
b There are two students in the same grade as Soo-Jin.   Y   N   DS
c Soo-Jin's grandmother wants Soo-Jin to finish her education.   Y   N   DS
d Shanae's grandmother can't read or write at all.   Y   N   DS
e Soo-Jin likes going to school with her grandmother.   Y   N   DS

3 **Answer the questions about Soo-Jin's and Shanae's grandmothers.**

	Soo-Jin's Grandmother	Shanae's Grandmother
a How much can she read and write?		
b Why did she have to leave school?		
c Why does she want to learn to read better?		

Digging Deeper

4 📖 **Write notes in the story map.**

Story Map

Setting

_____
_____
_____
_____
_____

Characters

_____
_____
_____
_____
_____

Plot: Beginning

_____
_____
_____
_____
_____
_____
_____
_____
_____

Plot: Middle

_____
_____
_____
_____
_____
_____
_____
_____
_____

Plot: End

_____
_____
_____
_____
_____
_____
_____
_____
_____

5 📖 **Mark (✔) the theme of the story.**

a   Life is difficult in a small Korean town.   ☐

b   Education is important for everyone.   ☐

c   Harvest time is more important than education.   ☐

Personalization

6 **Would you like your grandparents to be in school with you? Why or why not?**

_____
_____
_____
_____

How can we make our dreams come true?

Key Words

1 **Preview the Key Words.**

| separate | sunrise | debate | unfair | peaceful |

| victory | march | perseverance | inequality | balcony |

2 **Match the Key Words to the words with the opposite meaning.**

1 peaceful   a loss
2 separate   b fairness
3 sunrise   c giving up
4 victory   d together
5 inequality   e violent
6 perseverance   f sunset

Pre-reading

3 **Read the title and look at the pictures on pages 27–31. Circle the correct options. (There may be more than one.)**

1 What is the text about?

   a dreams   b Martin Luther King, Jr.   c growing up

2 What do you think the author's main purpose is?

   a to inform   b to entertain   c to persuade

3 What do you know about Martin Luther King, Jr.?

_____

4 **Listen and read.**

A Dream That Changed a Nation

By Kim Milne

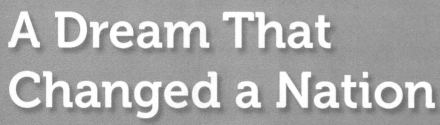

Statue of Martin Luther King, Jr., in Washington D.C.

Have you ever had a dream? Not the type of dream you have when you go to sleep at night, but something you wanted so badly that you put all of your time and energy into making it come true? Many people have dreams. Some people dream of becoming a pop star or making a music video with a million views. Others dream of being the first astronaut to fly to Mars or even becoming the leader of their country. But what if your dream was to change your whole society?

That was the dream of Martin Luther King, Jr. (MLK). It was a dream that seemed crazy at that time. His dream was to see that everyone in the United States of America was treated equally. This is the history of MLK, his fight to make his dream come true, and how he became one of the most important people in the history of the U.S.A.

Martin Luther King, Jr., was born in Atlanta, Georgia, on January 15, 1929. He had a younger brother named Alfred and an older sister named Christine. His father, Martin Luther King, Sr., was a pastor, and his mother, Alberta Williams King, was a teacher.

When MLK was born, slavery was no longer legal. It had been abolished by Abraham Lincoln in 1864. But life was still very hard for African Americans in the United States of America. They were treated like second-class citizens. Some lawmakers made special rules, especially in the southern states, to keep black and white people separate. These rules said that black and white people had to use different bathrooms, eat in different restaurants, and go to different schools and hospitals. And often the places for black people were not as nice as the places for white people. This separation of people of different colors is called segregation. When MLK was growing up, he experienced segregation every day. It was as normal to him as the sunrise.

Separate water fountains for white people and people of color

How would you feel if you couldn't use a water fountain or a swimming pool because of your skin color?

Segregated movie theater for African Americans

He also experienced prejudice from when he was young. (Prejudice means that you have an idea or opinion about someone because of the way they look or speak even if you haven't spoken to them or don't know them.) For example, when MLK was a little boy, he had a friend whose dad owned the store in front of his house. They played together all the time. But, when they were six, they had to go to different schools because his friend was white. After a while, his friend's dad wouldn't allow him to play with MLK anymore.

MLK was a very smart boy and did well in school. He skipped both 9th and 11th grade and finished high school when he was just 15 years old. He loved books and was on the school's debate team. When he was 14, he entered a speaking contest and won. But, while he was coming back home on a bus, he had to give his seat to a white person. This, along with many other experiences in his life, led him to understand that society had to change.

MLK's house

Boston University

In 1944, he went to Morehouse College to get a degree. After that, he decided to study religion at Boston University. Around the same time, he met Coretta Scott, a beautiful girl who was studying music. They fell in love and got married.

In 1955, MLK became a pastor at a church in Atlanta. There, he started to help his community to fight and change unfair laws. At this time, he also became interested in the ideas of Mahatma Gandhi. He had helped change India by leading peaceful protests. MLK wanted to do the same. So he talked with other leaders, and they decided to try to fight against discrimination in a non-violent way. He organized "sit-ins," a kind of protest where people sit down in a public place and refuse to move or leave. For example, people sat peacefully in segregated restaurants to protest segregation.

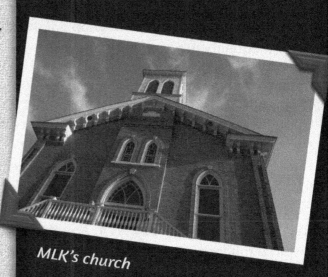

MLK's church

How would you feel if someone told you to give up your seat on a bus because of your skin color?

One day in 1955, in Montgomery, Alabama, a woman named Rosa Parks refused to give up her seat for a white man on a bus. The racist bus driver was furious and called the police. She was arrested and put in jail. MLK heard about this and went to Montgomery to help. He told everyone not to use the buses. For 381 days, all black people and a few white people stopped using them. The bus company lost a lot of money. Finally, the rules about public transportation were changed. This was a big victory, and it also showed many people that change can happen through peaceful protest.

The bus Rosa Parks was removed from

Over the next few years, MLK gave many speeches and participated in many marches to change unfair laws. He was arrested over twenty times. His house was bombed. But he never stopped. His hard work and perseverance earned him a lot of respect. He became a great leader for the people fighting to get rid of inequality in American society.

One of his most famous speeches was given in Washington, D.C., in 1963; 250,000 people marched from the Washington Monument to the Lincoln Memorial. MLK was the last person to speak to the huge crowd. He described the dream he had for all American people: that everyone should be treated equally and with respect. It is considered one of the most important speeches in American history. And it has inspired millions of people around the world ever since.

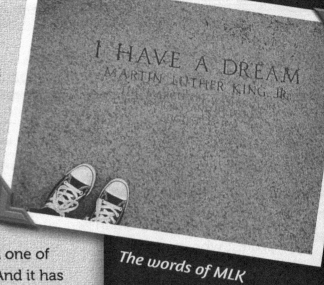

The words of MLK

In 1964, shortly after his speech, new laws were passed. Black and white people could now go to the same schools, restaurants, and hospitals. Discrimination was officially against the law. It was a great moment in American history, but for MLK it was only the beginning. He continued to fight peacefully. However, some people were not happy with the changes and wanted to stop him. On April 4, 1968, MLK traveled to Memphis, Tennessee, to help black garbage workers. They wanted to get the same money for doing the same job as white workers. Sadly, while he was standing on the balcony of his motel room, he was shot, and later died.

Statue of MLK in Birmingham, Alabama

MARTIN LUTHER KING JR. DAY (USA)

MLK helped to change many unfair things in the United States of America. He inspired thousands of people all around the world to fight for their rights in a non-violent way. He changed American history. Today, more than 50 years after his death, his memory lives on. Since 1986, every third Monday in January is a public holiday known as Martin Luther King, Jr., Day. It celebrates his life, his beliefs, and his never-ending fight to achieve his dream.

So what is your dream? What do you want to be? What do you want to do? What do you want to change? Whatever your dream is, if you persevere like MLK, you can make it come true—and you might make the world a better place.

Key Words

① **Complete the sentences.**

> debate   march   sunrise   balcony   unfair   victory

a   I woke up so early this morning that I was able to see the _____.

b   MLK felt that American society was _____ and tried to change it.

c   The protesters organized a _____ to demand more money for schools.

d   We won the soccer tournament. It was our team's greatest _____.

e   Our class had a _____ about where we should go on our next field trip.

f   We sat on the _____ and watched the people below us walking down the street.

Comprehension

② **Complete the timeline with the correct dates.**

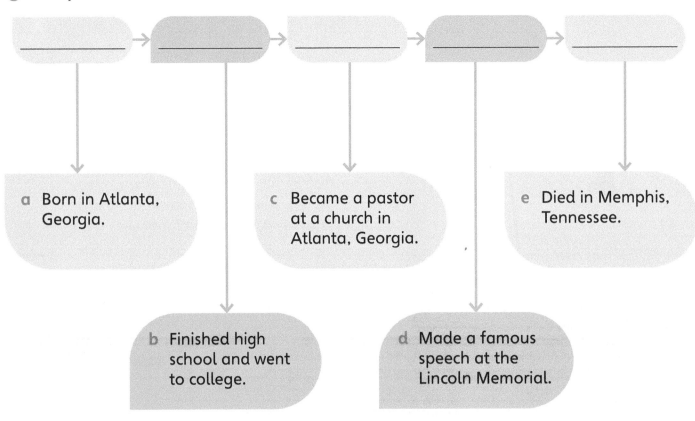

a   Born in Atlanta, Georgia.

b   Finished high school and went to college.

c   Became a pastor at a church in Atlanta, Georgia.

d   Made a famous speech at the Lincoln Memorial.

e   Died in Memphis, Tennessee.

③ **Which page of the text gives us the most information about MLK's ...**

a   early life?   _____

b   school?   _____

c   speeches?   _____

d   death?   _____

Digging Deeper

4 Look at your answers in Activity 3 on page 26.

a What do you think the author's main purpose is now? _____

b Were your predictions correct? _____

c What new things did you learn about MLK from the article?

_____
_____
_____
_____
_____
_____

d Is there any part of the text that tries to persuade you? What does it try to persuade you to do?

_____
_____
_____

5 Answer the questions.

a Why did MLK think it was important to lead peaceful protests?

_____

b What is a "sit-in," and why is it called that?

_____

c Why did people hold sit-ins in segregated restaurants?

_____

d Why is MLK's speech from 1963 important?

_____

Personalization

6 Write three of your dreams for the future.

_____
_____
_____
_____
_____

3 How can we deal with natural disasters?

Key Words

1 🎧 **Preview the Key Words.**
3.1

humidity   glacier   extreme   adjust   drizzle

refreshing   bulky   drenched   stranded   turbulence

2 **Read the definitions and write the Key Words.**

a water vapor in the air _____

b light rain _____

c unable to leave a place _____

d sudden movements of air _____

e very big and taking up a lot of space _____

f a large, slow-moving body of ice _____

Pre-reading

3 **Look at the pictures on pages 35–36 and answer the questions.**

a What does the boy look like? _____

b Where is he? _____

c When does this story take place? _____

d How do you know? _____

4 🎧 **Listen and read.**
3.2

A Quick Escape

By Steph Kilen • Illustrated by Ricardo Figueroa

"There's so much humidity here!" Arik said. "When are we going back to the floatasphere?"

"We're almost done for the day," his mom said as she lifted her binoculars to her face. "Just one more hour. Then, we can go back to camp where it is cooler, but you know we'll be staying here on land for another month."

Arik's parents were biologists. Every year his family spent three months on land, away from their home in the floatasphere. In school, Arik learned how, long ago, Earth had more land, before it was devastated by the melting glaciers. For the last 600 years, most people lived in floataspheres—enormous globes with controlled climates—because temperatures were too extreme on the land that was left. Plus, natural disasters, like tornadoes, volcanic eruptions, and hurricanes happened almost constantly. Many plants and animals had adapted to the changes, but humans hadn't. However, for a few months every year, people could still live on parts of the land. So, Arik's parents left their floataphere to study harpy eagles. To Arik, those months felt like forever. He missed his friends and fresh food. All their meals on land came out of packages and had a weird taste.

Arik sat down next to his dad, who was adjusting some cameras, and let out a sigh. His dad suggested he find his sister and go for a hike.

Arik climbed into the elevator. He found his big sister, Lena, reading on her Porta-Pad in a comfi-pod swing. He begged her to go with him because no one was allowed to go anywhere alone, not even the adults.

"Does it look like I want to go on one of your adventures?" Lena said.

"You can read all night!" Arik said. He knew what might change her mind: "I'll do all your chores tonight."

"Fine," Lena said.

The temperature was more comfortable on the ground because the rainforest's trees provided a lot of shade. A little happier now, Arik hiked along; Lena walked slowly behind. Then, the wind blew harder, and it started to drizzle. It was refreshing.

"Let's go back," Lena said.

Just then, the sky lit up, and a crash of thunder startled them both. There were never storms in the floatasphere. "Run!" Arik yelled, and they took off toward the tree fort.

Their parents were already on the ground with equipment in their hands when their dad shouted, "Here! Take these." He handed them each a Porta-Pad case, a pair of binoculars, and a backpack full of more things. "You got your wish, Arik. We have to pack quickly and return to the floatasphere. The experiments and studies are over. There's a hurricane coming!"

Hurricane season usually didn't start for another month. Their mom told Arik and Lena to wait there while they went back up to the fort to gather more equipment.

Arik and Lena took shelter under the fort, but the rain fell even harder. Arik had seen storms in movies, but they were much more terrifying in real life. Even through the trees, they could see the flashes of lightning. Thunder made the ground shake, and the wind howled. Arik and Lena looked at each other anxiously.

Soon, their parents returned. "Stay close!" their mom yelled to be heard over the noise of the storm. They couldn't run while carrying the equipment—it was too bulky—but they all went as fast as they could to camp.

Finally, soaking wet, they made it to the camp's main building. Dr. Kemper and Dr. Fernández, the other scientists, soon knocked on the door. They were drenched, too, and hurried inside.

"We took everything from the fort that we could carry," their mom said. "But we had to abandon some of our equipment. If we don't get to the heli-marine soon, we won't have enough time to get to the floatasphere."

"We already packed up our things," Dr. Kemper said. "We'll help with yours."

Lena and her parents ran around and put things in trunks while Dr. Kemper and Dr. Fernández turned on the camp's protection system. When they left, steel would cover the buildings to prevent rain from getting in through the walls and windows. But Arik was terrified; he started to panic. What if they were stranded there? What if the camp flooded?

"Arik! Come on!" his sister shouted.

"Lena, I ... ," he said.

"We're almost done," she said, "and then it will only take a couple hours to get home. If you help out, it will all go faster."

Arik thought about gaming with his friends and eating pizza; it was the motivation he needed to get moving. When all the equipment was collected by the door, they put on their waterproof suits to go back into the storm. Dr. Fernández started the heli-marine and opened the door. It took a couple trips, but eventually, all of the equipment and baggage was on the heli-marine. Arik and Lena's mom opened the door, and everyone took their seats. She was just about to shut the door when Arik noticed one box left outside. He ran to get it. "Arik! Come back! We have to leave, NOW!" his mom yelled. The heli-marine was making it even windier and noisier. Arik grabbed the box, being sure to hold it steady, and struggled against the violent wind to get back. "Hurry!" his mom said and helped him in.

Everyone had their safety belts on and earbuds in. Arik put the box under his seat and finally relaxed. "We can replace things, Arik, but we can't replace you," his dad said.

"I know. I'm sorry," Arik said. Still, he was happy he got to rescue the box. The earbuds blocked out all the noise, but they could talk into wristband microphones. The heli-marine bounced around in the turbulence as it flew higher. Arik closed his eyes, and Lena reached over and took his hand. "It's almost over," she said into her wristband, and Arik attempted a smile.

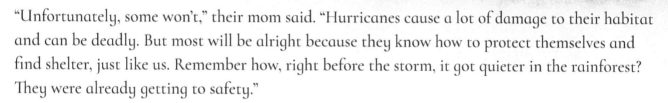

Then, suddenly, the ride was calm. "Look!" Dr. Kemper said and pointed to the video screen. A minute ago, the clouds blocked the camera's lens, but now they were high above the storm and could see the hurricane as it spun toward land.

"Will the birds and animals survive?" Arik asked.

"Unfortunately, some won't," their mom said. "Hurricanes cause a lot of damage to their habitat and can be deadly. But most will be alright because they know how to protect themselves and find shelter, just like us. Remember how, right before the storm, it got quieter in the rainforest? They were already getting to safety."

They all sat in silence for a while, relieved and catching their breath. Then, Dr. Fernández said, "It's too bad we didn't get more time to complete our research, though."

That's when Arik pulled his box from under his seat and opened it to reveal a terrarium, a glass container filled with dirt, tropical plants, some insects, and a tiny bright-green frog. "This is Frank," Arik said. "He's my pet, but maybe you could still study this micro-habitat since we had to leave the rainforest. Look in the little pond; some tadpoles are forming." He paused. "Plus, I know insects eat plants and frogs eat insects and harpy eagles eat frogs. That might help, too."

"So, being on land wasn't terrible, was it?" his mom asked.

Arik shrugged and smiled. Just then, they landed on the water. The heli-marine dove to enter the floatasphere's underwater doorway. A school of fish swam past the video camera. Arik's smile stretched across his face; it wouldn't be long now. "But it's always nice to be home," his mom said.

Key Words

1 Complete the sentences with the pairs of words.

> drizzle/refreshing   humidity/drenched   extreme/turbulence
> bulky/glacier   adjusted/stranded

a There was so much _____ in the jungle that I was _____ in sweat.

b The _____ ship slowly crashed into the enormous _____.

c They _____ the tent to stay dry; they didn't know how long they would be _____ on the island.

d The _____ on my face felt very _____.

e _____ winds caused _____, and the plane moved up and down in the sky.

Comprehension

2 Number the events from the story in order.

a The family makes it back to camp with some equipment. ☐

b Just before the heli-marine leaves, Arik runs out to get another box. ☐

c Arik is hot, bored, and thinking about his friends in the floatasphere. ☐

d They pack up their equipment to go to the heli-marine. ☐

e The heli-marine flies above the hurricane. ☐

f Arik convinces his sister to go for a hike, but a storm starts. ☐

g Arik arrives safely at the floatasphere with his family and his terrarium. ☐

3 Complete the sentences with the names of the characters.

> Arik   Lena   Arik's mom   Arik's dad   Dr. Kemper   Dr. Fernández

a _____ warns Arik that they have to leave quickly.

b _____ prefers reading to going on adventures.

c _____ offers to help the family pack their things.

d _____ realizes that being on land isn't that bad.

e _____ wishes they had more time to complete their work.

f _____ suggests that Arik and his sister go on a walk.

4 Why does Arik think that his terrarium might help the scientists study the rainforest?

_____

_____

Digging Deeper

5 📧 Imagine you are Arik when the hurricane begins. Write notes in the graphic organizer.

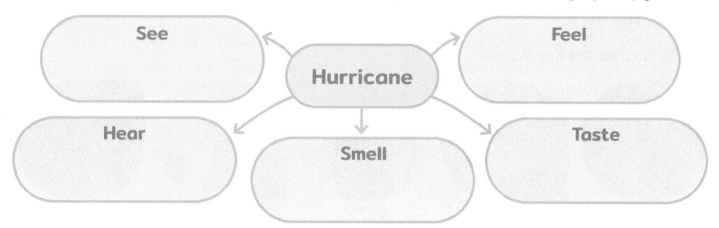

6 Complete the causes and effects.

Cause	Effect
Earth's glaciers melted.	a _____ _____
b _____ _____	Lena agrees to go for a walk with Arik.
The equipment was bulky.	c _____ _____
d _____ _____	Arik closes his eyes on the heli-marine.

Personalization

7 Circle an extreme weather event that happens in your country.

hurricane   flood   drought   tornado   blizzard

8 Answer the questions.

a How can people prepare for this event?

_____

_____

b What problems does it cause?

_____

_____

3 How can we deal with natural disasters?

Key Words

1 **Preview the Key Words.**
3.3

| powerful | erupt | bison | geyser | populated |

| tremor | record (v) | fortunate | economic | unpredictable |

2 **Read the definitions and write the Key Words.**

a very strong _____

b a spring of hot water that shoots up _____

c have people living there _____

d lucky _____

e a shaking or vibrating _____

f not possible to know in advance _____

Pre-reading

3 **Write one thing you know about each of these natural disasters.**

Volcanic Eruptions _____

Tsunamis _____

Earthquakes _____

Droughts _____

Tornadoes _____

4 **Listen and read.**
3.4

The Top Five Natural Disasters in History

By Paul Drury

A beautiful sunset, snow on top of a mountain, the sound of rain on the window: when we experience these things, we understand nature's beauty. We sometimes forget, however, that nature can also be dangerous. In a few seconds, a natural disaster can change the lives of hundreds of thousands of people. Even worse, it can cause the deaths of many thousands. To understand how powerful nature can be, let's take a look at five of the biggest natural disasters in history.

Type of Disaster: Volcanic Eruption
Where: Yellowstone National Park, U.S.A.
When: 640,000 years ago

This is Yellowstone National Park. Over four million people visit the park every year. (That's how many people live in Los Angeles.) It looks very peaceful, but it is actually a huge volcano. A long time ago, it erupted with a huge explosion. Scientists believe the eruption created a crater the same size as two Mexico Cities. It is hard to believe, but, underneath the trees, mountains, and bison, there is enough magma to fill 11 Grand Canyons. The volcano is still active, and that is why there are so many geysers and hot springs in Yellowstone. There's no need to panic, though. Scientists are confident that it's not going to erupt again in the near future.

Geyser

Yellowstone National Park

43

Type of Disaster: Tsunami
Where: Lituya Bay, Alaska, U.S.A.
When: July 9, 1958

What's the tallest building in your city? It's probably not as tall as the tallest tsunami was. The tsunami that hit Lituya Bay on July 9, 1958, was 520 meters high. That's more than one-and-a-half times higher than the Eiffel Tower. It's hard to imagine a wave that size. The tsunami began when an earthquake with a magnitude of 7.8 on the Richter scale hit the coast of Alaska. It caused a huge rockslide, and the subsequent tsunami completely destroyed all the trees up to 11 kilometers away from the coast. Luckily the wave hit a part of Alaska that was not highly populated, so very few people lost their lives.

Lituya Bay

Type of Disaster: Earthquake
Where: Valdivia, Chile
When: May 22, 1960

Have you ever stood near a busy road and felt the ground shake? It's a scary feeling! Everything moves, and you have no control. Maybe you've felt a tremor or, even worse, been in an earthquake. Scientists measure the strength of earthquakes using the Richter scale. The shaking caused by a truck going by is around two on this scale. When an earthquake measures five on the scale, some buildings may fall. At seven, the earthquake destroys most buildings over a large area. The biggest earthquake ever recorded occurred on May 22, 1960, in Valdivia, Chile. It measured nine and a half on the Richter scale!

Around 6,000 people died, and two million people lost their homes. The people of Valdivia say it was very fortunate that more people weren't killed. There was a small tremor before the earthquake hit. Very quickly, people left the buildings and stood in the streets where it was safer. It was the tsunamis the earthquake caused that killed most people. These tsunamis were so strong that people died on the other side of the Pacific Ocean, in the Philippines.

Valdivia after it was rebuilt

Dust storm

Type of Disaster: Drought
Where: The Great Plains, U.S.A. and Canada
When: 1931–39

The 1930s were a period of serious economic crisis in the U.S.A. Many people had no work and no money. During the same period, there was a severe drought that made it difficult to grow food. Therefore, many people suffered from hunger. In the worst year, 1936, many parts of the U.S.A. and Canada had the least amount of rain that they have ever had. The severe drought caused huge dust storms to develop. The storms swept across the Great Plains. Although people didn't know it at the time, they carried diseases. Already weak from hunger, many people could not fight off the diseases. In the end, over 6,000 people died in the two countries.

Type of Disaster: Tornado
Where: El Reno, Oklahoma, U.S.A.
When: May 31, 2013

The biggest tornado ever recorded occurred on May 31, 2013, in El Reno, Oklahoma. It was 4.2 km wide. That's the length of 3,000 buses! The winds inside the tornado reached a speed of 484 km/h. Compare that to the fastest train in the world, the Shanghai Maglev. It "only" travels at 430 km/h. What made things worse was that the tornado kept changing direction and speed unpredictably. And, everything lying in the tornado's path was destroyed.

Our planet is beautiful, but often dangerous. We have no way to prevent most natural disasters. And it is frequently impossible to predict them. What we can do is be prepared. Do your teachers talk to you about what to do if a natural disaster takes place? Do you know where to go and what to do? Acting quickly when disaster strikes could keep you safe. Make sure you're prepared!

Key Words

1 **Complete the sentences with the pairs of Key Words.**

> economic/unpredictable   records/tremors
> populated/bison   powerful/erupt

a A seismograph is an instrument that _____ earthquake

   _____.

b Today, Yellowstone National Park is _____ with around 5,000 wild

   _____.

c When _____ volcanoes _____, volcanic ash can travel
   great distances.

d _____ problems can be made worse by _____ natural
   disasters, which can happen at any time.

Comprehension

2 **Circle the correct options.**

1 The volcano in Yellowstone is ...

   a near the   b active.   c populated by
      Grand Canyon.   4 million people.

2 What can you find a lot of around Lituya Bay?

   a trees   b tall buildings   c people

3 What was the most dangerous thing about the Valdivia earthquake?

   a the small tremor   b the 9.5 earthquake   c the tsunami

4 Why couldn't people fight off disease during the drought on the Great Plains?

   a They were weak.   b They had no money.   c There were dust storms.

5 What best describes the tornado in El Reno?

   a fast, powerful, and   b fast, long, and   c fast, powerful, and
      explosive   powerful   unpredictable

3 **Write what the numbers refer to.**

a 4 million _____

b 520 _____

c 6,000 _____

d 2 _____

e 1936 _____

f 484 _____

Digging Deeper

4 In your opinion, which disaster was the worst? Give three reasons to support your opinion.

_____

_____

_____

5 🖼 Pick the best caption for the graphic sources that are relevant to the article.

1

   a The coast of Alaska is very far north.

   b The coast of Alaska experiences a lot of earthquake activity.

   c The coast of Alaska is home to a lot of wildlife.

2

   a Comparison of Richter scale levels

   b Largest earthquakes in history

   c How to survive an earthquake

3

   a How tornadoes work

   b Wind-resistant houses

   c A scale for measuring tornado strength

4

   a The Great Plains extend from Texas in the U.S.A. to Alberta in Canada.

   b The Great Plains are flat.

   c There are tornadoes on the Great Plains, too.

Personalization

6 Think about what people can do to prepare for natural disasters. Write one piece of advice for each.

a volcanic eruption _____

b tsunami _____

c earthquake _____

d drought _____

e tornado _____

4 What makes going to a show so exciting?

Key Words

1 🎧 **Preview the Key Words.**

clown   comedian   enter   juggle   somersault

kingdom   exit   tall tale   hospitality   reign

2 Match.

a a country whose ruler is a king or queen

b a complete turn or jump where people bring their feet over their heads

c a story that is false or difficult to believe

d to rule a country or have control over something

e being friendly and welcoming to guests

f a person who is funny or makes people laugh

comedian
hospitality
somersault
kingdom
tall tale
reign

Pre-reading

3 Look at the picture and text on page 49. Then, answer the questions.

a What type of text is this? _____

b How do you know? _____

c Where does the story take place? _____

d When does the story take place? _____

4 🎧 **Listen and read.**

The Twisted Tale of the Golden Goose

By Kim Milne • Illustrated by Axel Rangel

Scene 1

Narrator: The king's daughter, Moody, hasn't laughed for many years. The king has tried everything possible to make her laugh: mime artists, puppeteers, and comedies with special effects.

(Enter Clown riding a bicycle, juggling oranges, and balancing a spoon on his nose.)

(Enter Acrobat doing somersaults and falling over.)

(Courtiers and king are laughing, but Moody is not.)

King: Oh, well! Maybe next time! Thank you. *(waving people out of the court)*

Narrator: The king feels so desperate that he announces that whoever can make his daughter smile or laugh will receive a reward.

Characters
- Mrs. Abbott (mother)
- French Fry, Encyclopedia, Dobby (Mrs. Abbott's sons)
- King
- Moody (the king's daughter)
- Clown, Acrobat, Comedian
- Old Man
- 1st, 2nd, and 3rd friend
- Thief
- Policeman
- Bear

Scene 2

Narrator: Meanwhile, in the poorer part of the kingdom, Mrs. Abbott is talking to her three sons, French Fry, Encyclopedia, and Dobby. None of them knows anything about the king's problem.

Mrs. Abbott: Dobby, can you serve the soup, please?

Dobby: Yes, mother.

French Fry: Oh, no! Not that slimy snail soup again!

Encyclopedia: Well, you know, snails contain protein, fat, iron, calcium, vitamins A, B6, B12, and K. In fact, they are healthier than a whole egg.

French Fry: Yeah, yeah, but I still don't like them! They're too chewy!

Mrs. Abbott: OK, kids, listen. I need one of you to collect some wood from the forest tomorrow because we need it for our fire.

French Fry: I'll go, but only if you pack me a special lunch.

Mrs. Abbott: Of course I will, but you have to bring back two full sacks of wood.

French Fry: Yes, I will. I promise!

Scene 3

Narrator: The next day at court, the king invites the funniest man in all the kingdom to perform.

Comedian: Why do the French like snails?

Because they don't like fast food!

Moody: *(shaking her head)* He's terrible!

King: *(waving his hand for Comedian to leave)* Thank you, that's enough!

Scene 4

Narrator: In the forest, French Fry doesn't work at all. After making a bed with the softest leaves in the shade of a very old tall tree, he lies down and falls fast asleep.

(Enter Old Man.)

Old Man: *(banging his stick on the tree roots)* Ahem!

French Fry: *(jumping up)* Who are you? And what do you want?

Old Man: Could I have some food? I've been traveling for days, and I'm as hungry as a bear after a deep sleep!

French Fry: No way! These peanut butter and jelly sandwiches are the best in the world. So, definitely not!

Old Man: *(cupping his ears)* Where's the pot?

French Fry: *(getting angry)* No, I didn't say *pot*, I said *definitely not*.

Old Man: *(cupping ears again)* But I don't need a lot, just a small bite!

French Fry: *(shouting and angry)* Go away!

(Exit Old Man.)

Narrator: French Fry sleeps like a baby for the rest of the day. On his way home, a huge bear standing on its back legs and showing its teeth suddenly appears in front of him. Terrified, French Fry runs home as fast as he can.

Scene 5

(Enter French Fry.)

French Fry: *(out of breath)* Mother, you'll never guess what happened! I met an enormous bear on the way home. It must have weighed at least 400 kilograms and was about three meters tall. I'm sorry, but I dropped all the wood I collected.

Mrs. Abbott: Really? There haven't been any bears around here for years. Are you telling tall tales again, French Fry?

Encyclopedia: Yes, probably! I read that bears are an endangered species nowadays. And besides, you can't run faster than a bear; it runs as fast as a racehorse.

Mrs. Abbott: Encyclopedia, you'll have to go tomorrow!

Dobby: No, Mother! Let me go!

Mrs. Abbott: No, Dobby. Encyclopedia is going because he's older.

Encyclopedia: OK, then! Can you pack me a special lunch, too?

Mrs. Abbott: Sorry, there's no peanut butter left, but I have some freshly made lemonade.

Scene 6

Narrator: The king is running out of ideas.

(Enter King and courtiers with balloons tied to their ankles.)

King: Moody, look! You'll love this. It's called Balloon Stomp. We have to burst other people's balloons and protect our own at the same time. The last person with an inflated balloon wins.

Moody: OK. Three, two, one, go!

(The king and the courtiers are laughing hard, but Moody is not amused.)

Scene 7

Narrator: Back in the forest, Encyclopedia has finished collecting the wood and is just about to drink his lemonade when the old man appears.

(Enter Old Man.)

Old Man: Good afternoon! Can I have some of your lemonade? I've been traveling all day, and I'm really thirsty!

Encyclopedia: How do you know it's lemonade? It could be apple juice, strawberry milkshake, or even a Mango Julius Refresher, which, by the way, is my favorite. Anyway, no, you can't. I've been working very hard!

Old Man: *(cupping his ear)* Credit card? We're in the middle of a forest. And besides, I'm very poor.

Encyclopedia: Oh! Stop bothering me and go away! *(stands up angrily and exits)*

Narrator: On his way home, Encyclopedia also meets a huge bear on the road. Screaming, he drops all the wood and runs home.

Scene 8

Encyclopedia: *(enters running)* Mother! You won't believe what happened. I also met a bear. I'm sure it was an American Black Bear because it had a large body with thick legs, a large snout, and shaggy black hair. It flashed its claws at me.

Mrs. Abbott: What, another bear? I'm beginning to think you two boys didn't do anything at all.

Dobby: I wish I could go. I'd fight the bear.

Encyclopedia: I wouldn't do that if I were you. If you meet it, make yourself appear as big as possible by spreading out your arms and yelling as loud as you can. And don't climb a tree; they're great climbers!

Mrs. Abbott: I see—so, why didn't you do that?

Encyclopedia: I used my pepper spray and ran.

Mrs. Abbott: OK, Dobby. You can go, but be careful. But I can only give you some bread and water.

Scene 9

Narrator: Dobby works hard all day and collects two full sacks of wood. He then sits down and is just about to eat when the old man appears.

(Enter Old Man.)

Old Man: Good evening, Dobby. Would you mind sharing your lunch with a hungry old man?

Dobby: *(taking food from his backpack)* No, not at all, but it's only bread and water. Wait! I can't believe it—chicken and tomato pizza with extra cheese!

(He takes out a bottle.) No way, it's an orange creamsicle smoothie!

Old Man: *(eating and drinking)* This is really delicious. Thank you for your hospitality.

Dobby: You're welcome! This is the best pizza my mother has ever made!

Old Man: Oh, by the way, I left something for you inside the trunk of the big oak tree over there.

Dobby: Really?

Narrator: Dobby runs to the old oak tree and finds a golden goose in its roots. He turns around to thank the old man, but he has already left.

Scene 10

Narrator: So Dobby sets off for home with the two sacks of wood on his back and the golden goose under his arm, when suddenly some friends appear.

1st Friend: Hi, Dobby. What do you have under your arm? Wow, a golden goose! I would love one of its golden feathers. *(grabs a feather)* Oh, no! What's happening? I'm stuck!

2nd Friend: What do you mean "stuck"? Move over! I also want a feather! Oh, no! Now I'm stuck, too!

3rd Friend: *(grabbing 2nd Friend)* And me! Help! *(screaming)*

(All exit.)

Scene 11

Narrator: In another part of the forest, the king and Moody are going on their usual late afternoon ride. Suddenly they hear Dobby and the girls shouting in the distance.

King: What do you think all that noise is? *(gets off horse)*

Moody: Sounds like a fight ... Let's go and see.

(The king and Moody hide behind a tree.)

(Enter Dobby, the three friends, and the thief.)

Thief: Hello. Is that a golden goose? Get out of my way, girls! This is my prize!

Friends: Oh, no, it's not. It's ours!

Thief: *(pushing the girls)* No, it's mine! Oh, no. Now, I'm stuck, too!

(Enter Policeman blowing his whistle and running toward the thief.)

Policeman: There you are. I've been chasing you all day! Come here!

(grabs Thief and gets stuck)

(Moody and the king step out from behind a tree. When they see the king, everyone tries to bow, but they all fall down.)

Moody: *(laughing)* This is the funniest thing I have ever seen, father.

King: *(laughing)* Yes, I agree. Come to the castle young man, and I'll give you your well-deserved reward.

Dobby: Reward for what?

King: For making my daughter laugh, of course.

Dobby: But, I don't want a reward for making someone laugh.

King: As you wish! But, how about accepting some special royal mayonnaise to unstick all these people. I have some in my saddle!

Dobby: Really? Thank you so much, Your Majesty!

Narrator: Dobby covers all the stuck parts with the royal mayonnaise, and they immediately become unstuck. Dobby is now the city's hero. The king reigns over a happy kingdom once again. Of course, the Abbott family becomes very rich because, as everyone knows, a golden goose lays golden eggs every day. And what happens to the old man and the bear? Well, they are never seen again! And, of course, everyone lives happily ever after.

Key Words

1 Write the Key Words.

a Two types of people who try to make Moody laugh: _____,
_____

b Two activities that people try to make Moody laugh: _____,
_____

c Two stage directions: _____, _____

Comprehension

2 Number the summaries of the scenes in order.

a The king offers a reward to anyone who can make Moody laugh. `1`

b Dobby and friends make Moody laugh. The kingdom is happy again. ☐

c Mrs. Abbott decides to send Encyclopedia to collect wood the next day. ☐

d Dobby shares his bread and water. He goes to a tree and finds
a golden goose. ☐

e Encyclopedia returns home with no wood. Dobby volunteers to go
the next day. ☐

f Encyclopedia doesn't share his lemonade. He sees a huge bear and
drops his wood. ☐

g The Abbott family eats snail soup. French Fry says he will collect
wood for his mom. ☐

h Dobby takes two bags of wood and the golden goose home.
He meets some friends. ☐

i French Fry doesn't collect wood. He doesn't share his food and
runs home when he sees a bear. ☐

3 Write notes in the organizer about what happens to each character in the forest.

	What does he do in the forest?	What food does he have?	Does he share the food?	What happens next?
French Fry	goes to sleep →	peanut butter and jelly sandwiches →	no →	sees an enormous bear
Encyclopedia	→	→	→	
Dobby	→	→	→	

Digging Deeper

4 **Answer the questions about the story.**

a Why do you think French Fry and Encyclopedia get chased by a bear?

_____

_____

_____

b Why do you think the bread and water in Dobby's lunch change into pizza and a smoothie?

_____

_____

_____

c Why do you think Dobby's friends, the thief, and the policeman get stuck to the golden goose?

_____

_____

_____

d Why do you think the old man and the bear are never seen again?

_____

_____

_____

5 **Mark (✔) the best moral of the story.**

a Good things come to those who share. ☐

b Laughter is the best medicine. ☐

c Stay away from bears. ☐

Personalization

6 **Find three jokes or funny moments in the story and choose your favorite.**

7 **Write a joke you know.**

_____

_____

_____

_____

_____

4 What makes going to a show so exciting?

Key Words

1. Preview the Key Words.

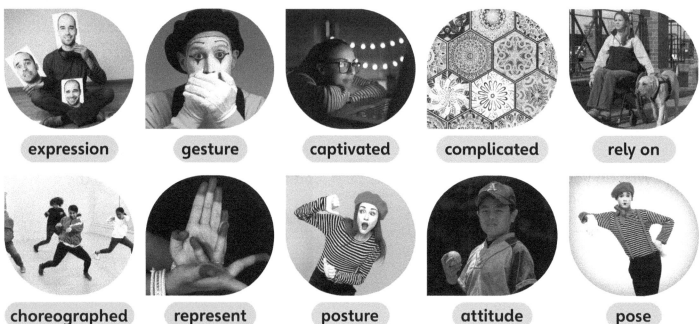

expression   gesture   captivated   complicated   rely on

choreographed   represent   posture   attitude   pose

2. Complete the sentences with the correct form of the Key Words.

a. She made a _____ with her hand to show us it was OK to come in.

b. We could tell he was upset by the _____ of his body.

c. The dance was very well _____. They moved together at exactly the same time.

d. Jack could tell by the _____ on Mike's face that he was very angry.

e. You can always _____ me to help you with your homework if you think it is too hard.

f. The photographer asked us to look natural and not to stand in a _____ for the picture.

Pre-reading

3. Read the title and look at the pictures on pages 59–61. Then, answer the questions.

a. What do you think "actions speak louder than words" means?

_____

b. Choose a picture. What action can you see? What is the person doing?

_____

4. Listen and read.

when Actions Speak Louder Than Words

By Robin Thompson

Have you ever wanted to be an actor or actress? Have you taken an acting class? If so, you will know that before actors and actresses speak a single line of dialogue, they learn how to mime.

But what is mime, and where did this popular art form come from? To "mime" is to act without speaking. Mime artists use facial expressions, gestures, and body movements to tell a story. The word *mime* or *pantomime* comes from ancient Greece. *Pantomimus* was a masked dancer who performed at Ancient Greek festivals. It is not known whether these shows were completely silent, though. The Romans later developed the art form. They invented "mummer plays" and "dumbshows." These Roman shows are closer to the type of mime we are familiar with today.

We see mime in theaters, in movies, and on streets all over the world. In places like Covent Garden in London, the historical center in Mexico City, and on the streets of Paris, it is common to see mime artists. You will find them surrounded by a captivated audience of children and adults.

Today, we are used to shows and movies with complicated special effects. So why do we still find mime so intriguing? Maybe it's because a good mime artist can make almost anything seem real—without props, dialogue, or special effects.

A mime artist performing in Paris

Mime in Movies

Before movies had sound, actors had to **rely on** facial expressions and body movements. Therefore, mime became very popular in silent movies. Charlie Chaplin was one of the first actors to use mime in his movies. He became one of Hollywood's biggest movie stars.

Charlie Chaplin as the Little Tramp

Rowan Atkinson as Mr. Bean

Mime is not used much in movies these days. However, there are still some exceptions. The character Mr. Bean is played by British actor Rowan Atkinson. Mr. Bean is a perfect example of how entertaining mime can be. It's the mime artist that makes the character so funny and interesting.

Mime and Dance

It's not just Hollywood that has used mime in movies. Bollywood movies from India are now famous around the world. Bollywood actors and actresses wear colorful costumes and perform in **choreographed** dances. These dance scenes also help to tell a story.

The classical dance of India, called *Bharatanatyam*, uses approximately 55 hand gestures. Each gesture **represents** a specific idea, event, action, or creature. These movements are called *mudras*. You can see some examples below.

This gesture represents the lotus, a type of plant.

This gesture represents a swan's beak.

Teach Yourself Mime

Want to try some mime for yourself?
First, learn to think like a mime artist.
Then, practice some basic moves.

Marcel Marceau was one of
the world's most famous mimes.

Use your body to talk. Instead of speaking, use facial expressions, gestures, and postures to "talk for you."

Practice in the mirror. Mime different facial expressions in the mirror to show emotions, attitudes, and reactions. Use a full-length mirror to perfect your body poses.

Use your imagination, If you really want your mime act to be realistic, use your mind before you use your body. Imagine a wall. Is it rough, smooth, wet, or dry? What color is it, and how high or low? Your body will react more naturally if what you imagine is more detailed.

Focus on a fixed imaginary point. Look at and point toward it. Move your body, but keep your hand and your eyes perfectly still. Later, try using two hands and create an imaginary surface. Move your hands along the surface, but keep your body still. It will look like you are moving along the side of a wall. Then, try pulling on an imaginary line. You will look like you're pulling on a rope.

Make things out of thin air. Mime makes almost anything possible. Try this! Hold your hand out at your side. Bend your fingers slightly. Move your hand up and down. You're suddenly bouncing an invisible ball!

With enough imagination, you can make all kinds of objects and situations come to life. You can jump over walls, climb stairs, and even get caught in the rain. That is the art of mime.

1

2

3

4

Key Words

1 Complete the text with the correct form of the Key Words.

Theater Review

The highlight of the evening was the mime artist.
The audience was (a) _____ by his
fascinating routine. It was incredible how he told the story
through facial (b) _____ and hand
(c) _____ alone. It was just him on the stage,
with no (d) _____ props or lighting, no words,
and only his movements to (e) _____ ideas.
Even the youngest children watching knew what feelings and
(f) _____ he was expressing.

Comprehension

2 Answer the questions.

a Who developed plays that were similar to modern mimes? _____

b Which actors are famous for using mime in movies? _____
_____

c What do dances and hand gestures help to do in Bollywood movies? _____
_____

d What two things do you need to use to teach yourself mime? _____
_____

3 Look at the three areas associated with mime in the organizer and categorize the words.

Bharatanatyam   The Little Tramp   pantomimus
mummer plays   Mr. Bean   choreographed

Movies or TV	Theater or Shows	Dance
_____	_____	_____
_____	_____	_____

4 Pick two of the numbered pictures on page 61. Describe what action the mime is representing.

Picture ☐ _____
Picture ☐ _____

Digging Deeper

5 📖 **Use your answers from Activities 2 and 3 to help you write a one-sentence summary for each section of the text.**

a History of Mime

_____

_____

b Mime in Movies

_____

_____

c Mime and Dance

_____

_____

6 **Match the steps to the activities for teaching yourself mime.**

l Use your body to talk.

2 Practice in the mirror.

3 Use your imagination.

4 Focus on a fixed imaginary point.

5 Make things out of thin air.

a Create a scene. Is it hot, cold, wet, or dry? Are you happy or sad?

b Hold out your hand with your palm down and pretend that you are bouncing a basketball!

c Communicate with your face, hands, or the way you sit or stand.

d Make different faces to yourself: laugh, smile, or look angry or surprised.

e Move your body but not your eyes and hands.

Personalization

7 **Write what you think each gesture means.**

_____   _____   _____

_____   _____   _____

8 **Think of three gestures you use. Show them to a friend. Can they guess what they mean?**

5 How can we stay healthy?

Key Words

1 🎧 **Preview the Key Words.**
5.1

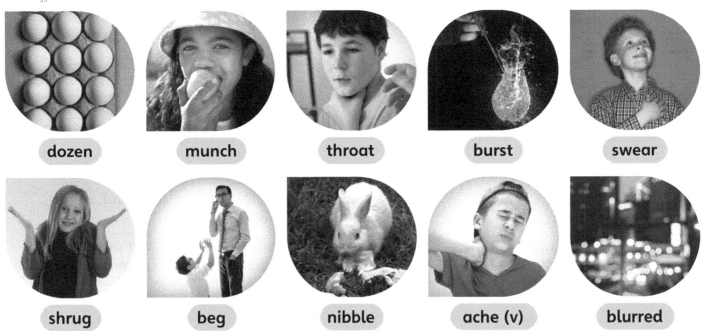

| dozen | munch | throat | burst | swear |

| shrug | beg | nibble | ache (v) | blurred |

2 **Complete the sentences with the correct form of the Key Words.**

a He _____ his shoulders because he didn't know the answer.

b The bubble _____ when I poked it with a needle.

c She coughed so much that her _____ was really sore.

d My neck _____ yesterday because I was staring up for a long time.

e The boy was _____ an apple loudly.

f We _____ Dad to let us have ice cream, but he said no.

g Amy _____ that she wouldn't tell anyone our secret.

Pre-reading

3 **Look at the titles of the poems and the pictures on pages 65–67. Make predictions.**

a What are the poems about? _____

b Are the poems funny or serious? _____

c How do you know? _____

4 🎧 **Listen and read.**
5.2

You Shouldn't Eat a Dozen Birthday Cakes

By Kenn Nesbitt
Illustrated by Flor Aguilar

You shouldn't eat a dozen birthday cakes.
You shouldn't drink a hundred chocolate shakes.
You shouldn't down a thousand piles of fries,
Or try to munch a million pizza pies.

You shouldn't lick a billion lollipops.
You shouldn't taste a trillion lemon drops.
You shouldn't drink your soda from a hose,
Or juice until it's shooting from your nose.

You shouldn't eat your ice cream like a goat.
You shouldn't shove your sugar down your throat.
For, if you do, it might just make you burst.
So you should choose the fruit and veggies first.

Grape Juice

Apple Juice

Jake, Who Only Ate Cake

By Kenn Nesbitt
Illustrated by Flor Aguilar

There was a boy whose name was Jake.
The only food he ate was cake.
For breakfast, lunch, and dinner too,
he just ate cake. I swear. It's true.
While other children might partake,
at times, of someone's birthday cake,
it seems that Jake saw nothing wrong
with feasting on it all day long.

His parents simply shrugged and sighed,
for, even though they tried and tried,
they couldn't get their son to eat
a piece of bread or any meat.
They begged him, "Please, oh, pretty please,
just have a snack of fruit and cheese."
But Jake would always shake his head
and say, "I'll just have cake instead."

And so, he never tasted beans,
or broccoli, or salad greens.
He never ate a bit of beef,
or nibbled on a lettuce leaf,
or munched a crunchy onion ring,
or licked a spicy chicken wing,
or sniffed a single Brussels sprout,
or even peeked at sauerkraut.

He said, "These foods are not for me.
I will not eat a pear or pea.
I don't see any reason why
I ought to try an apple pie,
a pickle, a potato chip,
a casserole, a spinach dip,
a sandwich, or a piece of steak,
when nothing tastes as good as cake."

It wasn't long till eating cake
turned out to be a big mistake.
Without some vegetables or fruits,
or meats, or seeds, or sprouts, or roots,
or any other healthy food,
he soon became a sickly dude.
His muscles ached. His vision blurred.
His stomach hurt. His speech was slurred.

He said, "I'd better climb in bed,
and have some cake to clear my head."
We haven't seen him since that day.
He might be dead. I couldn't say.
There's just one thing we know for sure;
if he's alive, we have a cure:
Instead of eating only cake,
try something else for goodness sake!

Key Words

1 **Complete the sentences.**

| blurred | nibbled | shrugged | swear | dozen | burst |

a There are a _____ eggs in this cake!

b There is a mouse in the garden. It _____ on the lettuce before it ran away.

c The dirt on her glasses _____ everything she looked at.

d I _____ that I haven't eaten any candy in weeks!

e Don't blow any more air into the balloon. It's going to _____.

f When I asked her who took my pen, she _____ and said she didn't know.

Comprehension

2 **Answer the questions.**

a What numbers are mentioned in the first poem? _____

b What does the first poem say you should eat before sweet food? _____

c What snack do Jake's parents offer him? _____

d Why does Jake prefer cake to other foods? _____

e If Jake is alive, what should he do? _____

3 **Complete the graphic organizer with foods from the poems.**

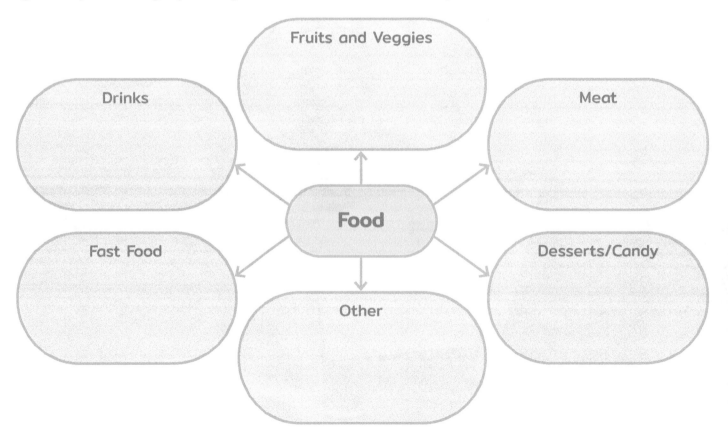

Digging Deeper

4 Complete the graphic organizer and answer the questions.

Clues in the Text	+	My Knowledge or Experience	=	My Inferences
a Why will the foods "make you burst" in the first poem?				
	+		=	
b Why does Jake eat more cake when he feels sick?				
	+		=	

5 Look at the advice in the first poem. Write advice for the people in the second poem.

Jake

Should	Shouldn't
a _____	_____
b _____	_____

Jake's Parents

Should	Shouldn't
a _____	_____
b _____	_____

Personalization

6 Use the foods in the story to create two meals you would eat.

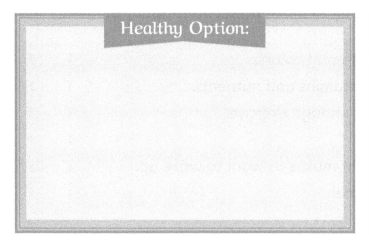

Healthy Option:

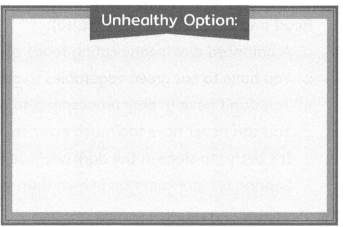

Unhealthy Option:

5 How can we stay healthy?

Key Words

① 🎧 **Preview the Key Words.**
5.3

obesity · cholesterol · appetizing · boredom · cramp

abdomen · endurance · insomnia · expose · snore

② **Write a Key Word with a similar meaning.**

a not excited: _____

b pain in your side: _____

c sleeplessness, wakefulness: _____

d strength, persistence: _____

e belly, stomach:_____

f uncover, show: _____

Pre-reading

③ 📖 **Use your knowledge about staying healthy to make predictions about the text. Read and circle *T* (true) or *F* (false).**

a A balanced diet means eating foods of different colors.	T	F
b You have to eat green vegetables to get vitamins and nutrients.	T	F
c You don't have to play team sports to get enough exercise.	T	F
d You can never have too much exercise.	T	F
e It's better to sleep in the dark because light makes us want to wake up.	T	F
f Snoring is more common in men than women.	T	F

④ 🎧 **Listen and read.**
5.4

Staying Healthy: Just Ask the Experts

By Ivor Williams

Dr. Lynn Harman

Prof. Gabrielle Smith

Do you want to know how to stay healthy? We brought together three experts—in the fields of diet, exercise, and sleep—to answer questions from kids just like you.

Let's meet our experts: Doctor Lynn Harman is an expert in nutrition and has worked with children and teenagers for many years. Gabrielle Smith is a professor of exercise science and has written many bestselling exercise guides for young people. And, Doctor Halil Tekin is one of the world's most respected experts on the subject of sleep.

 Now, let's see what they have to say about your questions.

Dr. Halil Tekin

Why do some people—like me—really like sweet things? And are they really that bad for us? (Paola from the U.S.A., 11 years old)

Dr. Harman: It's in your DNA! If you have more sweetness taste buds, you have a sweet tooth. Also, you prefer sweet things because you eat them often. If you grow up with fond memories of sweet foods—Grandma's cookies, for example—you connect sweetness with pleasant feelings. Remember, too much sugar can cause problems like diabetes, obesity, and high blood pressure. Sugary foods also cause tooth decay. So, try to eat less sugar, especially the extra sugar in cookies, breakfast cereals, pasta sauces, and processed foods.

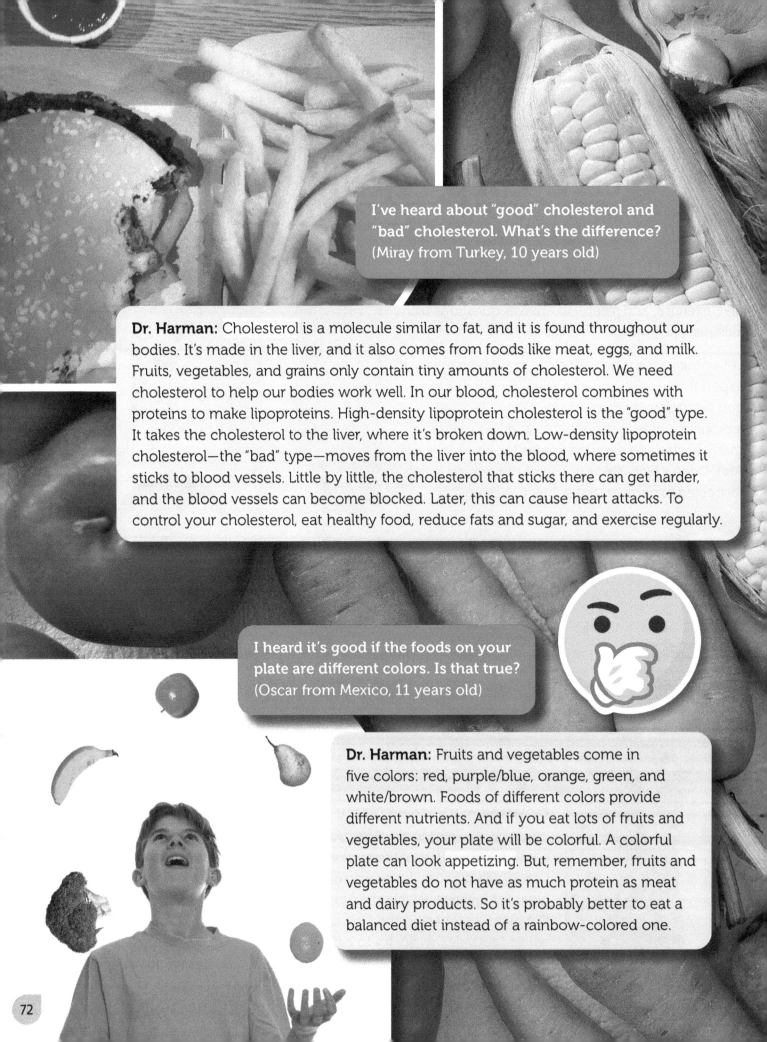

I've heard about "good" cholesterol and "bad" cholesterol. What's the difference?
(Miray from Turkey, 10 years old)

Dr. Harman: Cholesterol is a molecule similar to fat, and it is found throughout our bodies. It's made in the liver, and it also comes from foods like meat, eggs, and milk. Fruits, vegetables, and grains only contain tiny amounts of cholesterol. We need cholesterol to help our bodies work well. In our blood, cholesterol combines with proteins to make lipoproteins. High-density lipoprotein cholesterol is the "good" type. It takes the cholesterol to the liver, where it's broken down. Low-density lipoprotein cholesterol—the "bad" type—moves from the liver into the blood, where sometimes it sticks to blood vessels. Little by little, the cholesterol that sticks there can get harder, and the blood vessels can become blocked. Later, this can cause heart attacks. To control your cholesterol, eat healthy food, reduce fats and sugar, and exercise regularly.

I heard it's good if the foods on your plate are different colors. Is that true?
(Oscar from Mexico, 11 years old)

Dr. Harman: Fruits and vegetables come in five colors: red, purple/blue, orange, green, and white/brown. Foods of different colors provide different nutrients. And if you eat lots of fruits and vegetables, your plate will be colorful. A colorful plate can look appetizing. But, remember, fruits and vegetables do not have as much protein as meat and dairy products. So it's probably better to eat a balanced diet instead of a rainbow-colored one.

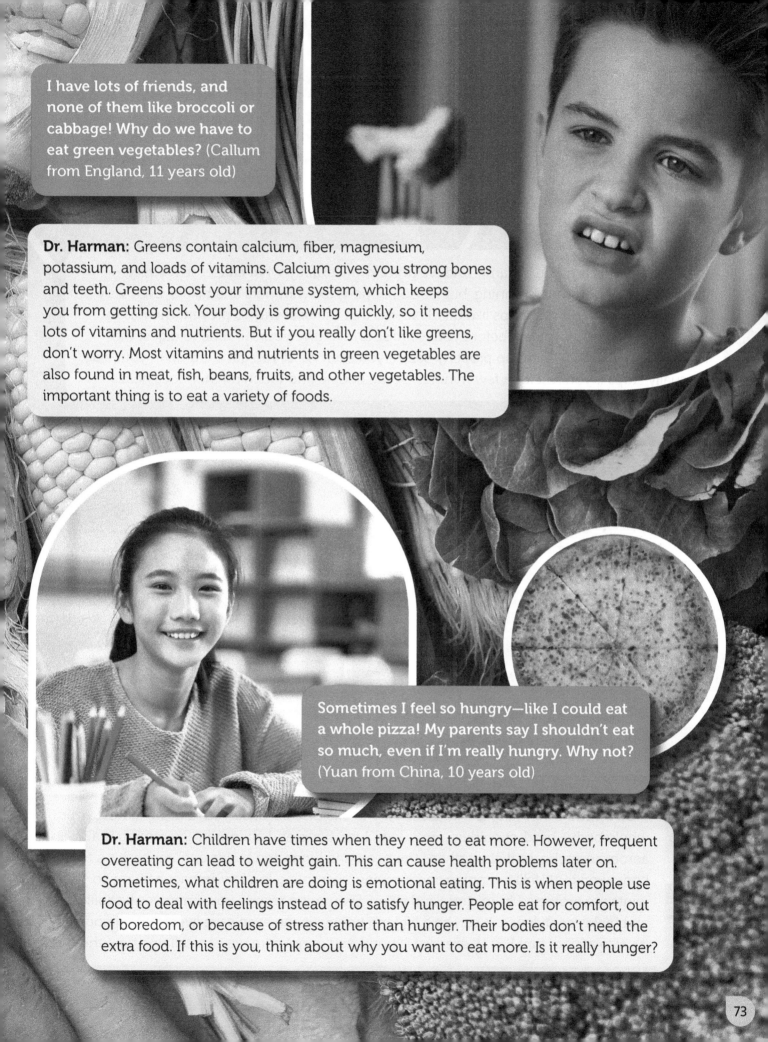

I have lots of friends, and none of them like broccoli or cabbage! Why do we have to eat green vegetables? (Callum from England, 11 years old)

Dr. Harman: Greens contain calcium, fiber, magnesium, potassium, and loads of vitamins. Calcium gives you strong bones and teeth. Greens boost your immune system, which keeps you from getting sick. Your body is growing quickly, so it needs lots of vitamins and nutrients. But if you really don't like greens, don't worry. Most vitamins and nutrients in green vegetables are also found in meat, fish, beans, fruits, and other vegetables. The important thing is to eat a variety of foods.

Sometimes I feel so hungry—like I could eat a whole pizza! My parents say I shouldn't eat so much, even if I'm really hungry. Why not? (Yuan from China, 10 years old)

Dr. Harman: Children have times when they need to eat more. However, frequent overeating can lead to weight gain. This can cause health problems later on. Sometimes, what children are doing is emotional eating. This is when people use food to deal with feelings instead of to satisfy hunger. People eat for comfort, out of boredom, or because of stress rather than hunger. Their bodies don't need the extra food. If this is you, think about why you want to eat more. Is it really hunger?

Sometimes, when I run a lot, I get a sharp pain in my side. Why? (Fernanda from Mexico, 11 years old)

Prof. Smith: This is called a cramp, and we don't know exactly what causes it. It's very common in long-distance running, but it also happens to swimmers and bikers. Even very healthy athletes can get cramps like this. It seems that the best way to prevent them is to limit how much food you eat before you exercise and to give yourself time to digest the food you do eat. Also, warm up properly before you exercise. If you get a cramp in your side, it usually stops if you rest for a few minutes. Some people find touching their toes helps.

My PE teacher says swimming is the best exercise. Is that true? Why? (Diego from the U.S.A., 10 years old)

Prof. Smith: Swimming is a fantastic way to exercise because you're using almost your whole body—head, shoulders, arms, legs, hips, back, and abdomen. Swimming is also an aerobic exercise, so it strengthens the heart and lungs and builds endurance. It's a total body workout! Unlike running and jumping, swimming is a low-impact activity, so your joints are protected from stress and strain. Swimming relaxes you, improves flexibility, and builds confidence. It can be a lifelong hobby; it can even save lives; and, of course, it's also a lot of fun! But all exercise is good, so I'm not sure we can call one type the best.

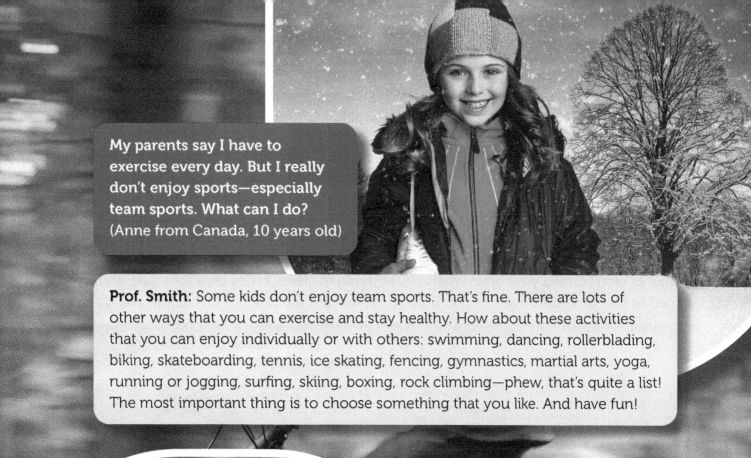

My parents say I have to exercise every day. But I really don't enjoy sports—especially team sports. What can I do? (Anne from Canada, 10 years old)

Prof. Smith: Some kids don't enjoy team sports. That's fine. There are lots of other ways that you can exercise and stay healthy. How about these activities that you can enjoy individually or with others: swimming, dancing, rollerblading, biking, skateboarding, tennis, ice skating, fencing, gymnastics, martial arts, yoga, running or jogging, surfing, skiing, boxing, rock climbing—phew, that's quite a list! The most important thing is to choose something that you like. And have fun!

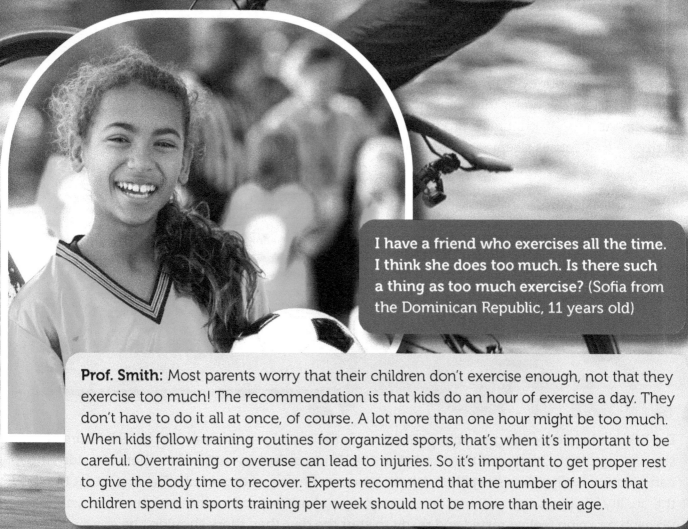

I have a friend who exercises all the time. I think she does too much. Is there such a thing as too much exercise? (Sofia from the Dominican Republic, 11 years old)

Prof. Smith: Most parents worry that their children don't exercise enough, not that they exercise too much! The recommendation is that kids do an hour of exercise a day. They don't have to do it all at once, of course. A lot more than one hour might be too much. When kids follow training routines for organized sports, that's when it's important to be careful. Overtraining or overuse can lead to injuries. So it's important to get proper rest to give the body time to recover. Experts recommend that the number of hours that children spend in sports training per week should not be more than their age.

Some nights I just can't fall asleep even though I'm really tired. Other nights I fall asleep right away. Why? (Michael from Australia, 11 years old)

Dr. Tekin: The inability to sleep is called insomnia, and there are various causes, including anxiety, nightmares, stress, major life changes, and your physical surroundings. See if these suggestions work for you: 1) Write in a journal before bedtime. This clears your mind so that thoughts won't crowd your brain when you're trying to sleep. 2) Get on a schedule, and try to go to bed at the same time every night. 3) Exercise earlier in the day, not just before you go to sleep.

I can't sleep unless my room is completely dark. Why does light stop me from sleeping? (Alex from the U.S.A., 10 years old)

Dr. Tekin: When our eyes are exposed to light during the night, this tricks our brains into thinking that it's time to wake up. As a result, our brains produce less melatonin—a hormone that causes sleepiness. To sleep well, your bedroom should be as dark as possible, with no lights on.

My mom says that someone my age should get 10 hours of sleep a night, but I never sleep that long. Is she right? (Nori from Japan, 11 years old)

Dr. Tekin: Many experts agree with your mom. Some say 11 year olds should get 9.5 hours of sleep every night. Others put the number at 10–11 hours. Just as with adults, there are kids who can function well on less sleep than others. You may be one of those kids. The important thing is the quality of your sleep, not just the quantity. If you have a good bedtime routine, and you wake up each morning feeling rested and ready to start the day, then there shouldn't be any problem.

My teacher says that if we spend a lot of time looking at screens—phones, tablets, etc.—before going to bed, we'll have problems sleeping. Is that true? (Nour from Egypt, 10 years old)

Dr. Tekin: Checking your phone just before you sleep distracts you. It stimulates your brain, and it keeps you awake. The blue light from screens and phones confuses your brain because it's similar to sunlight. It interferes with your body's internal clock. Stop screen time one hour before going to bed. If you want to read in bed, read a print book instead of looking at a screen. You'll sleep better.

Both of my parents snore very loudly at night. But my sister never snores, and she says I never do. Do adults snore more than kids? (Regina from New Zealand, 11 years old)

Dr. Tekin: Yes, snoring is much more common in adults than in children. People are more likely to snore if they sleep on their backs; it's more common in men than in women; and it's more likely to happen with people who are overweight. Snoring is usually caused by your tongue, mouth, throat, or airways in your nose vibrating as you breathe. It happens because these parts of the body relax and become narrower when you sleep.

What great questions, and what great answers! Please send in more questions for our experts! **And stay healthy!**

Key Words

1 Write the Key Words in the correct categories according to the text.

> insomnia   cramp   cholesterol   obesity   snore
> endurance   appetizing   abdomen

Diet	Exercise	Sleep
_____	_____	_____
_____	_____	_____
_____	_____	

Comprehension

2 Circle the correct options.

1 What is one cause of obesity?
    a too much sugar   b exercise   c insomnia

2 What don't green vegetables do?
    a make you sick   b help your immune system   c give you strong teeth

3 How is swimming different from running?
    a It builds endurance.   b It is a low-impact activity.   c It uses your arms and legs.

4 If you are 11 years old, how many hours per week should you exercise?
    a 15   b 12   c 11

5 Which one is not a cause of insomnia?
    a exercise   b stress   c nightmares

6 What can cause sleep problems?
    a melatonin   b the blue light from a phone   c darkness

3 Read the problems and write the solutions.

a You have a cramp in your side. _____

_____

b You don't like team sports. _____

_____

c You can't sleep after reading on a tablet in bed. _____

_____

Digging Deeper

4 📖 **Complete the graphic organizer with the new things you learned.**

	Diet	Exercise	Sleep
What or how much do you need?			
What is something you shouldn't do?			
What is something you should do?			

5 **Give advice to the following people.**

a Someone who eats lots of candy every day.

_____

b Someone who never exercises.

_____

c Someone who only sleeps for six hours a night.

_____

Personalization

6 **What can you do in each area to improve your own health?**

a Diet _____

b Exercise _____

c Sleep _____

6 Why is language special?

Key Words

1 🎧 **Preview the Key Words.**
6.1

| capture | stationary | soar | circular | driftwood |

| mangrove | horizon | riverbank | ripple | fluorescent |

2 **Answer the questions.**

a   Where can you find driftwood? _____

b   What is an example of something that is circular? _____

c   What is the opposite of *stationary*? _____

d   What makes a ripple in water? _____

e   What is an example of something that soars? _____

f   What is another word for *fluorescent*? _____

g   What is the opposite of capturing something? _____

Pre-reading

3 **Look at the pictures on pages 81–85. Write a question about each story element.**

a   The Characters: _____

b   The Setting: _____

c   The Events: _____

4 🎧 **Listen and read.**
6.2

Jaynie of the Daintree

By Kate Fitzgerald • Illustrated by Israel Ramírez

It was beginning to rain when Tim and his uncle Ernie left Sydney. It was summer vacation, and they were traveling to the Daintree Rainforest in Cape Trib, located at the northern tip of Australia. Ernie was a wildlife photographer, and he was so excited to be taking his nephew with him. They were going to take pictures of saltwater crocodiles. Tim had seen one that had been captured, in the zoo. But he had never seen a wild one.

Tim watched the raindrops fall. Their plane was stationary for the moment. Ernie communicated via sign language, "We'll be soaring above the clouds soon. There's always blue sky above the rain."

Tim didn't want to leave his friends because, like him, they were deaf. He was worried he wouldn't hang out with anyone he could communicate with—except for his uncle—the whole summer.

Above the clouds, the rain stopped, and Ernie moved his hands to sign, "I just know you'll make friends in the Daintree, mate."

Tim smiled. It was like Uncle Ernie knew exactly what he was thinking sometimes.

Their hotel was a modern treehouse with glass walls. They stared out on a variety of trees in every shade of green. Tim closed his eyes and felt the coolness of the forest's air against his cheeks. He lay down on his bed to read a comic book until it got so dark that he couldn't see the words.

The next morning, Tim woke up when his cell phone started to vibrate. It was a message from Uncle Ernie—a smiley face and an ice cream emoji followed by two question marks. Tim laughed and sent back a smiley face and three exclamation points.

They drove to the ice cream store. Rows of perfectly spaced trees shaded colorful picnic tables. Tim looked up at the trees and saw a girl with wild red hair sitting on a branch. "Strange," he thought.

When they arrived, there was no one around. Perhaps they had gotten there too early for ice cream. Suddenly, the girl from the trees appeared. "G'day. What would you like?" she asked. Tim looked at Ernie. Lip-reading was easy when he could see a person's lips and facial expressions, but the girl was blocking her face from the sun. Ernie put his hand on Tim's shoulder.

"Hi! I'm Ernie, and this is my nephew, Tim. Tim's deaf, so you need to look at him and speak clearly so he can see what you're saying. He uses sign language if you know any?"

"I'm so sorry, I don't," the girl apologized, looking directly at Tim and speaking clearly. "I'm Jaynie. My family owns this place. So, you want ice cream for breakfast?"

Tim smiled and pointed to the sign that read: *Ask about today's special!*

Jaynie listed strange fruits: "We have black sapote and soursop."

Ernie used the sign language alphabet to spell the flavors out—the words were complex and certainly not flavors they'd tried before. Tim signaled for two servings, and they both agreed it was delicious ice cream.

Ernie finished his ice cream and asked Jaynie, "Do you know how we can find the creek? I'm here to photograph the crocodiles."

"Incredible! Can I come? I'm fascinated by crocodiles!" Jaynie smiled.

"You should ask your parents," Ernie said, and Jaynie ran across the orchard and found her mom, who came over to meet Tim and Ernie. They chatted awhile, and Jaynie's mom gave permission for her to go to the creek. As they walked to the car, Tim held up his phone to Ernie who said "Of course! You two can text, too." Tim and Jaynie exchanged numbers, and Jaynie put a crocodile emoji next to Tim's name, which made him laugh.

Jaynie shouted: "Pull over!"
Ernie stopped the car suddenly.

"Come on!" Jaynie yelled. She found a big stick and banged it on the ground as she walked.

Tim sent her a message. "What's that for?"

She asked Ernie: "What's the symbol for "snake" in sign language?"

Ernie bent his index and middle fingers and moved them in a circular motion. Tim jumped back, scanning the ground.

Jaynie texted a snake and "I'm scaring the snakes!" Tim gave a nervous nod to say "yes."

The trail led to a beautiful beach that was huge, flat, and surrounded by a dense forest. It was empty, which made it seem a little mysterious. The only moving things were the waves of the ocean.

Ernie spoke and signed, "Stay away from the water's edge. Crocodiles inhabit this area."

On the way to the boat, Tim jumped at every piece of driftwood—they were all shaped like crocodiles! Jaynie couldn't stop laughing. "Did you know baby crocs chirp like birds before they hatch?" she texted. "And they hiss like snakes when danger approaches!"

They looked for crocodiles for hours. Every time they thought they'd seen a crocodile, Ernie looked through his binoculars, but it was always just mangroves. As the sun sank below the horizon, Ernie stopped the motor. An enormous crocodile lay on the riverbank. It was as stationary as a statue. Ernie grabbed his camera and started photographing.

Suddenly, the crocodile noticed them. It opened its mouth slowly, showed them sixty-four sharp teeth, and entered the water.

"Where did it go?" whispered Jaynie.

The water was very still. They all held their breath.

Jaynie and Ernie stared forward, searching for the crocodile. But out of the corner of his eye, Tim saw ripples begin to appear near the boat and two eyes looking back at him out of the water— they were like fluorescent green grapes.

Tim waved his arms around trying to get the attention of the other two as they continued to stare in the other direction. There was no time. The crocodile was almost at the side of their boat. Tim started the motor, and the boat jumped forward, making Ernie and Jaynie fall backward.

As Ernie stood up, he saw the crocodile and Tim's panicked face. He stopped the boat and raised his camera just in time to capture the crocodile jumping in the air and landing exactly where their boat had been sitting.

"Nice work Tim! That photo will be on the cover of a magazine for sure!" said Ernie.

Tim and Jaynie were silent, their mouths wide open, until Jaynie started to laugh, followed by Tim.

Tim fell asleep as they drove back to Jaynie's house.

"Do you ever wish Tim could hear?" asked Jaynie.

Ernie thought about her question and smiled. "No, I like him just like he is."

Jaynie liked that answer. "You're right. There's nothing wrong with being different."

From then on, every morning, the three of them would share tropical fruit in the car on their way to the boat. Ernie took photos while Tim and Jaynie searched for more crocs. During the afternoons, they'd all enjoy some ice cream. Tim taught Jaynie the alphabet in sign language, and Jaynie took Tim on the trails to show him the Daintree's wildlife.

Tim was incredibly sad when it was time to leave the Daintree. He texted Jaynie a sad face emoji, and she signed back "same."

Ernie found the pair of them and said to Tim, "Time to go, mate. But, what do you think about coming back next summer?"

Jaynie and Tim gave each other a huge high five.

Key Words

1 **Complete the text with the correct form of the Key Words.**

| capture | mangrove | riverbank | horizon | soar | ripple |

We pushed the boat away from the **(a)** _____ and floated silently down the dark river. The water was still, except for **(b)** _____ coming from the paddles or flies landing on the surface. Suddenly, there was a movement, and the guide pointed to the left. Something was climbing out of the water into the **(c)** _____ forest, and I lifted my camera to **(d)** _____ it. I was too late. Whatever the creature was, it disappeared into the forest, and our boat moved on. A few moments later, the river opened out onto the ocean. The bright light hurt my eyes as I looked at the **(e)** _____ in the distance and saw an eagle **(f)** _____ overhead.

Comprehension

2 **Write the answers to your questions from Activity 3 on page 80.**

a _____

_____

b _____

_____

c _____

_____

3 **Answer the questions.**

a Why doesn't Tim want to leave his friends?

_____

b Why can't Tim understand what Jaynie is saying when she first speaks to him?

_____

c Why does Jaynie bang a stick on the ground?

_____

d What time of day is it when they see the crocodile? How do you know?

_____

e How do we know that Ernie had a successful trip?

_____

f Do Tim and Jaynie have trouble communicating? Why or why not?

_____

Digging Deeper

4 📧 **Read the sentences and write the corresponding stage of the plot.**

| beginning | rising action | climax | falling action | resolution |

a They see a huge crocodile on the riverbank. It disappears into the water, and then Tim sees ripples near the boat. He can't get the others' attention, so he starts the motor just in time.

_____

b Uncle Ernie captures a photo of the crocodile jumping out of the water and landing where the boat had been. They all start laughing, and Jaynie and Tim become friends.

_____

c Jaynie, Tim, and Uncle Ernie walk through the rainforest to a beach and then cruise on a boat through mangroves for hours, looking for crocodiles.

_____

d Jaynie shows Tim the trails in Daintree, and Tim teaches Jaynie sign language. He is sad to leave, but Uncle Ernie suggests coming back next year.

_____

e Tim and Uncle Ernie go to Daintree to look for crocodiles. Tim doesn't want to leave his friends. When they get there, they meet a girl named Jaynie.

_____

5 **Complete the Venn diagram with ways of communicating in the story.**

Jaynie   Both   Tim

Personalization

6 **Describe how Ernie makes the sign for a snake.**

_____

_____

_____

_____

7 **Make your own sign language. Choose three animals and draw or describe signs you can make with your fingers, hands, or body.**

| crocodile | bird | dog | rabbit | fish | lion |

6 Why is language special?

Key Words

1 🎧 Preview the Key Words.
6.3

compose | integrate | inhabitant | variation | invade

settle | influence (v) | etymology | derive | jumble

2 **Match the Key Words to their meanings.**

1 derive	a	enter with force
2 influence	b	be a part of something
3 invade	c	come from
4 settle	d	affect things or people
5 compose	e	a messy mixture
6 etymology	f	a word's historical origin
7 jumble	g	stay and live in a place

Pre-reading

3 **Complete the chart with two things you know and two things you want to find out about the English language.**

Things I Know	Things I Want to Find Out
a _____	a _____
b _____	b _____

4 🎧 **Listen and read.**
6.4

Where in the World Does English Come From?

By Adam Critchley

Did you know that English is composed of many languages? That's because English grew by adopting words from other languages. As you learn English, you will discover many words that come from French, German, Arabic, Chinese, Norwegian, Hindi, and even languages spoken by Native Americans.

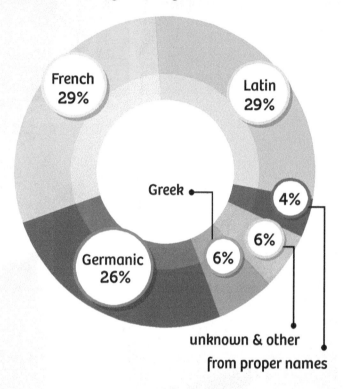

Origin of English words

French 29%
Latin 29%
Greek
4%
6%
6%
Germanic 26%

unknown & other
from proper names

So how did so many words from other languages become part of English? There are two main reasons. England, where the English language originated, was populated by different peoples from different countries over time. These people brought their own languages with them, and they mixed with the languages already spoken in England.

The English language also picked up words from other languages as a result of English people traveling to foreign countries. They traveled to many parts of the world and came back with new words. Also, English became the first language in new places and integrated some of the words from the languages spoken by the people there. To find out more, let's look at the history of the English language.

English: A Short Summary of a Long History

The original language spoken in the British Isles was Celtic, the language of the Celts, who were the islands' original inhabitants. Over time, the Celtic language split into different groups. Variations of Celtic languages are still spoken today, in Wales, Ireland, and Scotland, and also in parts of northern France. Very few words with a Celtic origin remain in the English that we speak today, but you may recognize a few, like *bin*, *dad*, and *brat*.

Britain was invaded by the Romans in 55 BCE, and England, Wales, and part of Scotland became part of the Roman Empire. The Romans spoke Latin, and Latin words entered the language at this time. Only a few have remained in use, like *mountain* and *tower*. And the names of some English cities, like Manchester, were formed around the Roman word *castra*, which means "camp."

Hadrian's Wall marked the northern border of Roman control in Britain.

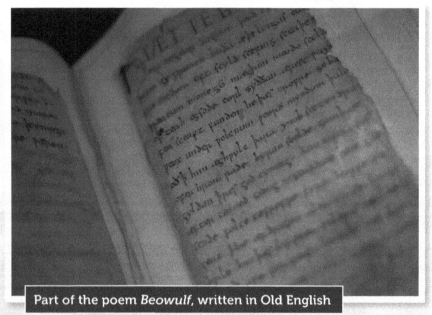

Part of the poem *Beowulf*, written in Old English

Britain remained part of the Roman Empire until the mid-5th century CE, when a group of people we now call Anglo-Saxons came to settle in Britain from Germany. The language they spoke is Old English. This was the earliest version of the English language we speak today. Old English began to replace the Celtic and Roman languages spoken in the British Isles. A lot of the words and features in contemporary English come from Old English, for example, a lot of the plural forms and irregular verbs. That's why we say *men* and not *mans* and *drank* instead of *drinked*. However, around 85% of the words in Old English are no longer used in contemporary English.

Did You Know?

More English words begin with the letter *s* than any other letter.

Then, Latin influenced English again because it was brought back to Britain by missionaries who came from Rome in the 7th century CE. Examples of Latin words that entered English at this time are *language*, *picture*, *quiet*, and *school*.

A Viking longship

Did You Know?

Sentences that contain all 26 letters of the alphabet are called *pangrams*. One of the shortest pangrams in English is "The quick brown fox jumps over the lazy dog." Can you write another one?

Around the year 865 CE, Britain was invaded by the Vikings, who came from Scandinavia. They spoke a language called Old Norse. The Vikings tried to integrate with the people in Britain, and they adopted the English language. Nonetheless, there are around 1,000 words in English that have Old Norse origins, such as *anger*, *bag*, *get*, *happy*, *sky*, and *take*.

In 1066 the Normans, who came from France, invaded Britain, and French became the official language for almost 300 years. It was spoken by the rulers and the upper classes. As a result, many French words made their way into the English language, such as *action*, *castle*, *restaurant*, and *omelet*.

A scene from the Bayeux Tapestry, which depicts the Norman invasion

The Canterbury Tales written in Middle English

Did You Know?

One interesting result of the Norman invasion is that, in English, the word for an animal, like *cow* or *chicken*, has its origin in Old English. But the word for the food from that animal, like *beef* or *poultry*, comes from French. Can you guess why this is so?

However, most people in Britain continued to use English, ensuring that the language survived. English became the official language again in 1362. Old English evolved into Middle English, which was spoken until the 15th century, and gradually became Modern English, the language we speak today.

Farther from England

In the 16th and 17th centuries, explorers and colonists from England started to explore the world on ships. And, over time, many new English settlements were established in places like North America, South America, India, and Africa. As the English people traveled to these places, they started to adopt the words that were used there.

A bandana

Therefore, many of the words of foreign origin in English do not seem foreign at all because they have been in use in English for hundreds of years. But their origins might surprise you. When you look up a word in a dictionary, you can discover its origin. The origin of a word is called its etymology, which is also the name for the study of the origins of words.

Let's look at the origins of some common words in English: Some words from German in English are *kindergarten, noodle,* and *hamster*!

Sanskrit is the language of ancient India. Words of Sanskrit origin in English include *bandana, cheetah,* and *jungle*.

"Checkmate!"

Did You Know?

The word *checkmate* that we use in chess comes from the Persian phrase *shāh māt,* which means "the king is helpless."

Hindi is one of the many languages spoken in India. Hindi has given many words to English, such as *dinghy,* which is a small boat, *pajamas,* and *bungalow*.

Some of the Arabic words that have passed into English are *algebra, cotton, lemon, lime,* and *orange*.

Did You Know?

There is no word in English that rhymes with *orange.* Don't believe it? Just try to think of one!

Spanish brought words into English such as, *canyon, coyote, mosquito,* and *patio*.

Many English words are also derived from Greek, for example, *antique, athlete,* and *grammar*.

Words of Chinese origin that we use in English include *ketchup, tea,* and *typhoon*.

The Grand Canyon in Arizona, U.S.A.

Some words in English are derived from languages spoken by the native inhabitants of the Americas. *Kayak*, for example, comes from Inuit, the language spoken by the people of the North American Arctic. Further south, from the Mayan language spoken in Mexico, Guatemala, and Honduras, came *hurricane*. And, from Náhuatl, the language spoken by the Aztecs, came *tomato*, *chili*, and *avocado*.

One Language or Many?

As you can see, from the beginning, English has always been a jumble of several languages. And, like all languages, English is a living language. It is constantly growing and adding new words, especially now that global communication is faster and easier than ever before.

Even though English is the official language in about 40 countries, it is not the world's most-spoken native language. (A native language is a language that you speak from birth.) Can you guess which language that is? That's right! It's Chinese, which has 1.3 billion native speakers. English is not even the second-most spoken language in the world; that's Spanish, with 460 million native speakers. English has 379 million native speakers, about 38 million more speakers than Hindi.

You may not be surprised to hear that English is the language that is learned as a second language by the largest number of people. So you are not alone in studying English! About 1.5 billion people, or around one-fifth of the planet's population, speak English!

Key Words

1 **Complete the entries in the etymology dictionary with the Key Words from page 88.**

a _____

(n.) "one who lives in a place," late Middle English: from Old French, from Latin *inhabitare* "to live in."

b _____

(n.) "difference," late 14c., from Old French *variacion* "diversity," directly from Latin *variare* "to change."

c _____

(v.) "come to rest," Old English *setlan*, "cause to sit," from *setl* "a seat."

d _____

(v.) "to bring together the parts of," 1630s, from Latin *integrare*, "make whole," from *integer* "whole, complete."

Comprehension

2 **Read and circle *T* (true) or *F* (false).**

a The English language originated in different countries around the world.	T	F
b The Anglo-Saxons brought Old English to Britain from Germany.	T	F
c Old Norse was spoken by kings, queens, and the upper classes.	T	F
d Modern English started to appear in the 15th century.	T	F
e During the 16th and 17th centuries, English integrated words from around the world.	T	F
f There are more native speakers of English than any other language.	T	F

3 **Number the events in order.**

a Britain was invaded by the Romans. ☐

b The Vikings invaded Britain. ☐

c Middle English changed into Modern English. ☐

d People on the British Isles spoke Celtic. ☐

e The Normans invaded Britain. ☐

f Exploration led to integration of new words from around the world. ☐

g Anglo-Saxons settled in Britain. ☐

h English became the official language. ☐

Digging Deeper

4 📖 **Read the statements and write _F_ (fact) or _O_ (opinion).**

a   More English words begin with the letter _s_ than any other letter.   _____

b   The origins of some words in English are surprising.   _____

c   Britain remained part of the Roman Empire until the mid-5th century CE.   _____

d   It is interesting that we have words for animals from Old English
and words for food from French in contemporary English.   _____

e   Words of Chinese origin that we use in English include _ketchup_,
tea, and _typhoon_.   _____

f   About 1.5 billion people, or around one-fifth of the planet's
population, speak English!   _____

5 📖 **Find two more facts from the text and complete the chart with your opinions
about them.**

	Fact		Opinion
a	_____	a	_____
	_____		_____
b	_____	b	_____
	_____		_____

6 **Read the "Did You Know?" boxes again. Research another interesting fact about
English for your own "Did You Know?" box.**

Did You Know?

Personalization

7 **Read the lists of English words that derive from other languages on pages 92–93. Are
there any English words that you use in your native language? Which ones?**

_____

_____

8 **Write a reason why it is important for you to learn English.**

_____

 How do machines help us?

Key Words

1 🎧 **Preview the Key Words.**
7.1

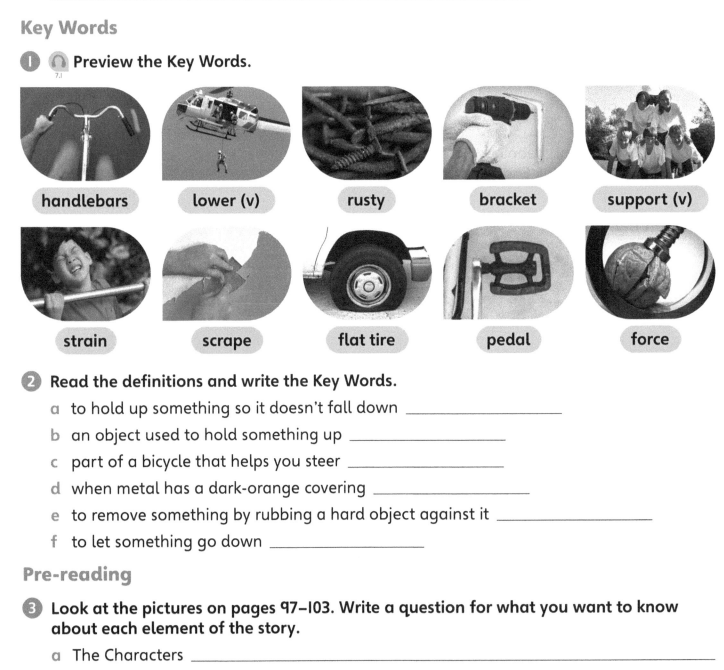

handlebars   lower (v)   rusty   bracket   support (v)

strain   scrape   flat tire   pedal   force

2 **Read the definitions and write the Key Words.**

a to hold up something so it doesn't fall down _____

b an object used to hold something up _____

c part of a bicycle that helps you steer _____

d when metal has a dark-orange covering _____

e to remove something by rubbing a hard object against it _____

f to let something go down _____

Pre-reading

3 **Look at the pictures on pages 97–103. Write a question for what you want to know about each element of the story.**

a The Characters _____

_____

b The Setting _____

_____

c The Plot _____

_____

4 🎧 **Listen and read.**
7.2

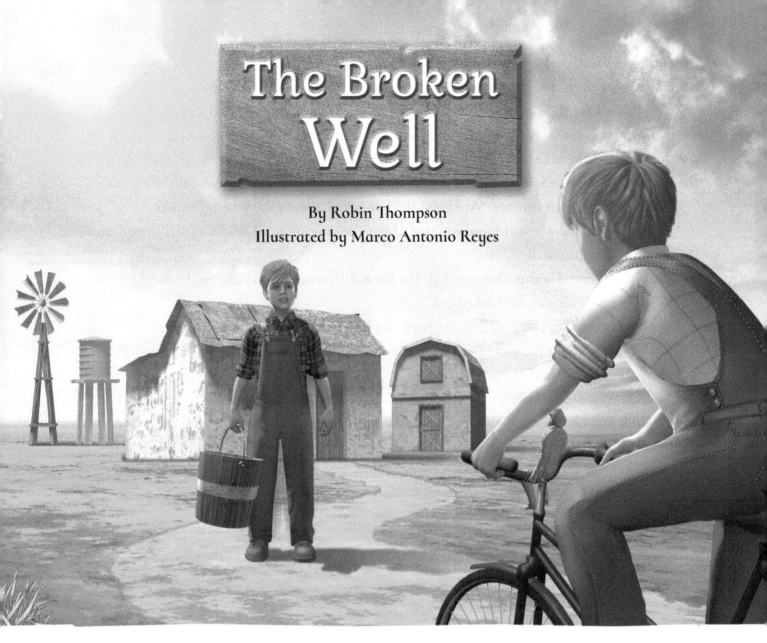

The Broken Well

By Robin Thompson

Illustrated by Marco Antonio Reyes

L ife on the Great Plains was never easy, and life on the Great Plains during the Great Depression of the 1930s was even worse. There was nothing "great" about any of it, thought Toby as he waited at the edge of the ranch for his little brother, Jed.

The ranch looked old and dull. The walls needed fresh paint, and the old water pump needed to be replaced—then Toby wouldn't need to walk every day to the well to get fresh drinking water for the family. There was no chance that would happen soon, though, because there was only just enough money for them to live day to day. Fixing the ranch would need to wait.

Jed rode toward Toby on his old bicycle. He skidded to a stop, and the wooden action figure dressed like a cowboy that sat on top of the bike's handlebars fell to the ground. Toby picked it up, cleaned it, and handed it back to his brother.

"Sorry, Captain," said Jed to his wooden friend as he sat the toy figure back on the handlebars.

"Come on," said Toby. "Let's go get this water."

He started walking, carrying an empty bucket at his side, and Jed followed, riding in circles around Toby as they went.

Jed raced ahead on his bike, riding around loose pieces of stone that covered the ground. They were once part of the old drinking well.

"Careful!" shouted Toby as Jed reached the well, but it was too late. Jed lost control of the bike as its front wheel hit a large piece of fallen stone. Jed crashed into the wall of the well. He fell to the ground, and the bike fell on top of him. Once again, Jed's precious wooden cowboy flew from the handlebars, and, a few seconds later, the captain hit the floor at the bottom of the well.

Toby ran to help his brother. "Are you OK?" he asked, lifting the bike off of Jed.

"I'm fine," said Jed. He was more worried about the captain, and he got up off the ground and looked down into the well.

Toby joined him. He was also worried, but for a different reason—the well was almost dry.

"What are we going to do?" asked Jed.

"There's nothing we can do. Let's just hope the rain comes soon."

"I don't mean about the water—I mean about the captain. We can't leave him there!"

"Are you serious?" said Toby.

The look on his little brother's face told him that Jed was totally serious.

The well, just like the ranch, wasn't in good condition. The handle that was once used to lower the bucket down into the well no longer worked. The rope was now just hanging over a rusty wheel, and the bracket that held it was ready to break at any time.

"There's no way I'm going down there, Jed. I'm sorry, but the wheel won't support my weight, and you're not strong enough to lower me down or pull me up again."

"We have to do something, Toby! I won't leave the captain alone in the dark!"

Toby covered his face with his hands and shook his head. He tied the water bucket to the end of the rope. Then, without warning, he grabbed Jed in his arms and threw him into the air, catching him on the way down as Jed screamed.

"Hey! What are you doing?" shouted Jed.

"Well, I'm too heavy, but you're as light as a feather, little brother. I think the wheel will hold your weight, and I just proved I'm strong enough to lift you."

Toby laughed, but Jed didn't. Toby lowered his brother to the ground and took the other end of the rope.

"Sit in the bucket," he said.

"No way!"

"You want to rescue your cowboy, don't you?"

Jed thought for a moment. He looked nervous, but then said, "OK, this is now an official rescue mission!"

Toby pulled the rope tight and slowly lowered the bucket, with Jed sitting in it, down into the well. He watched the wheel carefully. He was worried about the strain of Jed's weight. The sound of metal scraping against metal grew louder, but it looked like the pulley would hold Jed's weight at least.

"Are you OK, little brother?"

"Almost there," called Jed.

Then, suddenly, the rope went loose in Toby's hands, and he fell back onto the hard ground. A second later, he heard a bang as Jed and the bucket hit the bottom of the well.

"Jed!" screamed Toby, standing up and running to the well. He looked down into the hole, and could see his brother lying in the dark with the bucket by his side. The wheel above the well had held, but the bucket's handle had broken because of Jed's weight. "Are you hurt?"

Jed spoke quietly. "I'm OK, but my arm hurts. And I can't move it."

"I'm going to get Dad!" shouted Toby. "Stay calm, Jed. We'll get you out of there!"

Toby's first thought was to take Jed's bike and ride back to the ranch, but he saw that it had a flat tire. Instead, he ran as fast as he could.

Toby soon arrived back at the well with his dad. Toby's dad left the engine running as he jumped out of the old pickup truck and ran to the well. Toby was close behind.

"Son, can you hear me?"

"Hey, Dad," came the reply from below. "I think my arm's broken."

"Take the rope, Toby," said his dad. He ran back to the truck. "Tie the rope to the trailer hitch," he shouted.

"Dad, Jed won't be able to tie the rope around himself with a broken arm, or hold on to the rope for us to pull him out," said Toby. "But I have another idea!"

He ran to Jed's bicycle and dragged it toward the truck. "Do you have your tools, Dad?"

"You know me. I always have my tools!"

"Great!" said Toby excitedly. "We need to take the bike apart."

With the two of them working together, it took only a few minutes to completely take apart Jed's bicycle—the two wheels, the chain, and the pedals. Toby was left holding the metal frame. He turned it upside down so that his dad could put the rope through the hole where the pedals used to be.

"Jed," shouted Toby, "sit on the frame and hold on with your good arm."

Toby tied the other end of the rope to the truck's trailer hitch, and his dad backed the truck up to the side of the well, gradually lowering the bike frame down into the well.

Toby looked over the side of the well. He couldn't see much.

"OK," called Jed. "I'm on."

Toby signaled to his dad, who started to drive forward very slowly.

Jed must have only been a few centimeters off the ground when Toby shouted urgently for his dad to stop. The pulley didn't look like it could hold the weight of Jed and the bicycle frame. It was no good—the truck had to back up again and lower Jed down.

Toby and his father both thought hard.

Toby glanced all around, looking for something—anything—that could help, and then he saw the rest of the bicycle parts.

"Dad, can you cut some rope off? I think I know how we can do this."

Toby started pulling the flat tire off of Jed's bicycle wheel. "We can use the bicycle wheel as a new pulley system."

His dad didn't look convinced, but he cut some rope off anyway. Toby used the rope to tie the bicycle wheel to the bracket. Then, he put the other rope over the wheel to make a new pulley. He pulled on the wheel to check it was strong enough and smiled.

"This could work, Toby," said his dad.

Once again, Toby tied the rope to the truck, and his dad started the engine. The truck moved forward little by little. The rope became tight. There was a lot of force on the bicycle wheel, but it turned easily and supported Jed's weight.

Toby looked over the edge of the well and saw Jed coming up, sitting on the bike frame.

When Jed's head appeared above the top of the wall, Toby shouted to his dad, who stopped the truck. Toby held out his arms to lift up his brother, but before he could do so, Jed held out the wooden toy.

"The captain first," he said.

Toby laughed, rescued the captain from Jed, and then lifted Jed out of the well.

"I'm sorry," said Toby. "This was my fault." He was talking both to Jed and to his dad, who had run over to give both his sons a big hug.

"Ow! My arm!" shouted Jed.

"Oh, I'm sorry, Jed," said his dad. "We'd better get you home, then I'll go get the doctor to look at your arm."

"Don't worry about me," shouted Jed. "What about my bike?"

They lifted Jed's bike, piece by piece, into the back of the truck, and put Jed into the front seat.

"How do you feel?" asked his dad as they drove back to the ranch.

"Thirsty," said Jed.

Toby suddenly remembered why they'd gone to the well in the first place, and that the well was almost dry.

"Don't worry," said his dad, as if reading his thoughts. "It will rain soon. And, we have to get a new bucket."

Key Words

1 **Complete the text with the Key Words.**

> flat tire   support   strain   pedals   force

How to Ride Uphill on a Bike

Riding a bike is easy, but some hills are very steep. You may experience some **(a)** _____ from pedaling your bike uphill. First, you have to **(b)** _____ some of your weight on the handlebars and move them from side to side. Then, you have to press down on the **(c)** _____ with a lot of **(d)** _____ in order to move forward. Finally, you don't want any accidents on your ride. So, avoid any glass or nails on the ground that might cause a **(e)** _____.

Comprehension

2 **Number the events from the story in order.**

a   Toby has the idea of lowering Jed into the well in the bucket.

b   Toby makes another pulley using the bicycle wheel and gets Jed out of the well.

c   Jed falls and hurts his arm.

d   Jed rides his bike while Toby walks to the well.

e   Toby and his dad take apart the bike to make a pulley, but Jed is too heavy.

f   Jed has an accident on his bike and drops his toy down the well.

3 **Answer the questions.**

a   Why do Toby and Jed go to the well? _____

b   What does Jed want to get from the bottom of the well? _____

c   Why didn't Toby ride the bike to tell his dad about the accident? _____

d   Why did Toby throw Jed up in the air? _____

e   Why can't they use the well's pulley to rescue Jed? _____

f   How did the bike become useful? _____

4 **Label the parts of the pulley.**

> wheel   bracket   rope

Digging Deeper

5 Look at the questions you wrote in Activity 3 on page 96. Which ones were answered? Write the answers.

a _____

b _____

c _____

6 Complete the sentences.

a The story is set in _____ during _____.

b The two main characters are named _____ and _____.

c The main events in the plot are when Jed _____

and Toby _____.

d I think the theme of the story is _____.

7 📖 What connections can you make with the story? Complete the graphic organizer with your own ideas.

	Making Connections	
Connection to My Own Experience	**Connection to Another Story**	**Connection to the World**
When I read the words _____ it reminded me of _____ _____	The story reminded me of the book/movie _____ _____ because _____ _____	In this story I read about _____ It reminded me of _____ _____

Personalization

8 Imagine you were stuck at the bottom of a well for a few hours. What three things would you most like to have with you and why?

Item	Reason
_____	_____
	_____
_____	_____
	_____
_____	_____
	_____

7 How do machines help us?

Key Words

1 Preview the Key Words.

automation   intricate   efficient   install   pedestrian

surgery   mechanical   assist   incision   precision

2 Write the Key Words next to the words or phrases with the same meaning.

a put in place _____

b help _____

c accuracy _____

d very detailed _____

e machine-like _____

f well organized _____

g a cut in something _____

h a walking person _____

i having a machine do something _____

Pre-reading

3 Look at the pictures on pages 107–11. Predict what kinds of machines will be discussed.

a _____

b _____

c _____

d _____

e _____

4 Listen and read.

Will Everything Be Automated?

By Ivor Williams

Dr. Weissman

Today in *Technology Times*, we will listen to a conversation between two experts on automation and robotics. Dr. Cinthia Weissman is a historian of technology from the Western University of Technology. And, Dr. Patrick Dixon is a professor of engineering and robotics at Nikola Institute of Technology. Let's see what they have to say about the future of robotics and automation.

Dr. Dixon

Karel Čapek

Dr. Weissman: Hello, Dr. Dixon. Nice to meet you.

Dr. Dixon: Hello. I'm very happy to meet you as well.

Dr. Weissman: Well, to start off, did you know that we've only been using the word *robot* to describe self-controlling machines for about a hundred years? It comes from the Czech word, *robota*, which means "forced labor." Czech writer Karel Čapek used it in his play *R.U.R. (Rossum's Universal Robots)*.

Dr. Dixon: So the word *robot* isn't that old. But it was first used in a work of science fiction.

Dr. Weissman: Yes, but robots and automation are now facts of life. Robots make cars, TVs, washing machines, and thousands of other things. In the future, robots will be able to do much more than just build things. Many jobs might be automated. Lots of office jobs might be automated. That's because those tasks are very predictable and can easily be programmed. Other jobs might be harder to automate. Teachers, for example, will probably never be replaced by robots.

Dr. Dixon: So, do you think robots can bring benefits to the workplace?

A robotic vacuum cleaner

Dr. Weissman: Well, there are some benefits. Most workers don't enjoy doing repetitive tasks. They lose their concentration and get distracted, which can lead to errors or injuries. Robots are stronger, faster, and more accurate than humans. They never get tired, even when doing exactly the same thing over and over again. Robots can lift very heavy items, or they can perform small, intricate tasks. For repetitive tasks, robots can keep doing them and always at the same level of accuracy.

Robots making a car

Dr. Dixon: I see. But because robots are so efficient, a lot of people worry about unemployment. There won't be enough jobs for everyone.

Dr. Weissman: People are often afraid of new technology. But, you know, people said the same thing before, when machines were first introduced. And yet companies still needed people to do jobs. It's true that robots can replace workers. But the development of the new technology creates new industries and, in turn, more new jobs. So, jobs won't disappear. They will be different, though.

Dr. Dixon: I see. Let's talk about the cost, though. This is one of the biggest challenges for companies. It costs so much money to introduce robots into the workplace. Robots need humans to program and operate them. I'm sure that, for some companies, it's difficult to find skilled workers to fill these specialized roles.

Dr. Weissman: That's true, but once a company has bought and installed its robots, there are very few costs. Robots don't need paychecks, or lunch breaks, or vacations, or time off for being sick. You start them on a repetitive task. Then, as long as you maintain them, they keep working without a break.

Dr. Dixon: I can see the advantages of that.

Engineers repairing a robot

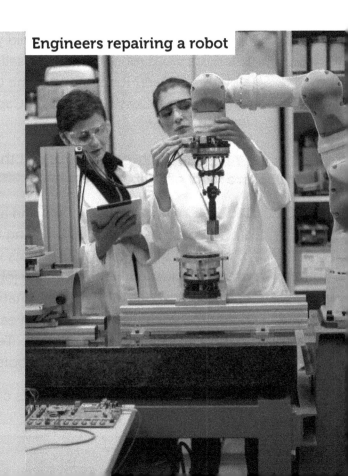

Dr. Weissman: Robots can also work in conditions that would be dangerous or impossible for humans. They can work in outer space, or they can work underwater. They can work in places that are extremely hot or extremely cold. They can handle dangerous chemicals, radioactive substances, or high-voltage electricity. Using robots helps to reduce risk to human workers.

Dr. Dixon: OK, I accept that robots might be better at some jobs, but there are some areas where they can't take over. They can't really improve their performance because they can't "think" for themselves. Robots can't cope very well in unstructured environments. They don't know the difference between right and wrong, and they find it hard to make choices in unexpected situations.

Firefighter using a drone

What a self-driving car might see

Dr. Weissman: For example?

Dr. Dixon: Well, let's look at self-driving cars. What if a robot has to choose between crashing into some pedestrians or crashing into a wall, which might harm the passengers inside the car? Are we comfortable with a robot making this choice?

Dr. Weissman: You're right. We still haven't worked out the answers to everything!

Dr. Dixon: We may never work out the answers to questions like that, but let's talk about robotic surgery. That's a particular interest of yours, isn't it?

Dr. Weissman: That's right. Robotic surgery allows doctors to perform many complex operations. The robotic equipment has a remote camera and mechanical arms with surgical instruments attached to them. The surgeon sits at a computer console and controls the arms. During the operation, other doctors assist the surgeon who is controlling the robot. Surgeons can treat patients without having to make large incisions in their bodies.

Dr. Dixon: It sounds great. What do you see as the main advantages?

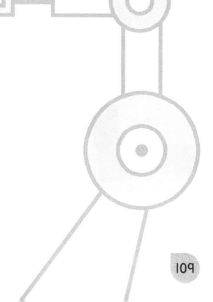

Dr. Weissman: Many operations need great precision. One slip of the surgeon's hand can cause serious harm to a patient. With robots, there is no shaking and there are no sudden movements. The doctor has greater control over the operation. Robotic surgery uses very small surgical instruments. These allow access to parts of the body that are usually difficult to reach. Robotic surgery gives the surgeon a magnified, high-definition, 3D view of what is happening inside a patient. This is a much better view than is normally possible.

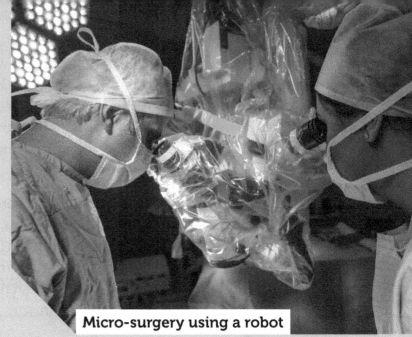
Micro-surgery using a robot

Traditional operations can sometimes take many hours. This is exhausting for surgeons, who have to be on their feet all that time. With robotic surgery, the surgeon can sit comfortably at the console while operating. This helps them to keep alert for the whole operation. And this reduces the chance of making a mistake because of tiredness.

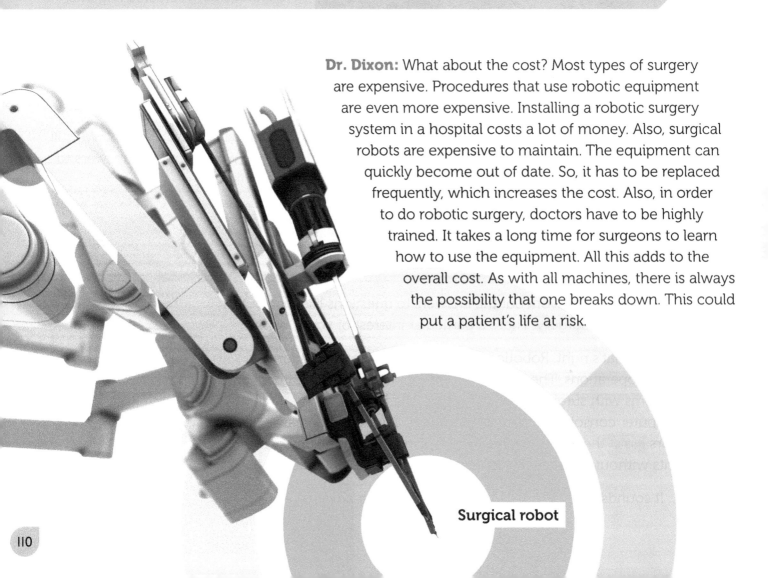

Dr. Dixon: What about the cost? Most types of surgery are expensive. Procedures that use robotic equipment are even more expensive. Installing a robotic surgery system in a hospital costs a lot of money. Also, surgical robots are expensive to maintain. The equipment can quickly become out of date. So, it has to be replaced frequently, which increases the cost. Also, in order to do robotic surgery, doctors have to be highly trained. It takes a long time for surgeons to learn how to use the equipment. All this adds to the overall cost. As with all machines, there is always the possibility that one breaks down. This could put a patient's life at risk.

Surgical robot

Dr. Weissman: Yes, it's expensive, but there are great benefits for patients. There are fewer complications during and after surgery. There's often less pain, and less blood is lost. Scars are smaller and less visible, and the risk of infection is reduced. The length of a patient's hospital stay is shorter, and their overall recovery is quicker.

Dr. Dixon: I can understand all of that, but I've also heard that some doctors experience other disadvantages. Some surgeons say that when they use the robotic arms, they lose the sense of touch that they normally have. They cannot feel the tissue that they are operating on, and what a tissue feels like conveys a lot of information to a surgeon.

In the end, I'm not sure that I would trust a robot with my life. What if something went wrong during a surgery? A trained surgeon has spent many years practicing medicine and can deal with unexpected occurrences. Will a robot that is programmed to do specific tasks be able to cope with something out of the ordinary? Part of what makes a good surgeon is that they have good judgment that they have developed over a lifetime of practicing medicine. You can't program a machine to have good judgment.

Will doctors use VR (virtual reality) during surgery?

Our future?

Dr. Weissman: That's true. I don't think robots will replace surgeons, but they will assist them. If you pair a good surgeon with a robot, the potential is enormous. Imagine, in the future, surgeons will be able to perform operations from a great distance. For example, an astronaut at the International Space Station could be treated from Earth using robotic surgery!

Dr. Dixon: That would be incredible! One thing is undeniable: we will be seeing more and more robots in our everyday life. But, we will have to wait and see how automated our lives become.

Key Words

1 Match the sentence parts.

1	Automation in factories can reduce	a	replace human arms and legs.
2	Robots can assist doctors	b	because robots are so efficient.
3	Mechanical limbs are used to	c	be safer for pedestrians.
4	Precision machines can	d	perform intricate tasks.
5	Self-driving cars might	e	be very expensive.
6	Installing robots in hospitals can	f	during surgery.
7	People worry about unemployment	g	the risks to some workers.

Comprehension

2 Circle the correct options. There may be more than one.

1 Robots are good in the workplace because they …

  a are unpredictable.   b are accurate.   c teach human workers.

2 When they operate mechanical arms on a console, surgeons …

  a get tired quickly.   b have greater control.   c make large incisions.

3 The costs of robotic surgery are higher because …

  a doctors need more training.   b equipment needs to be replaced frequently.   c patients stay longer in the hospital.

4 Dr. Weissman thinks that robots will eventually …

  a replace doctors.   b develop good judgment.   c treat astronauts in space.

3 Write three advantages and three disadvantages of automation.

Advantages	Disadvantages

4 Label the opinions *W* (Dr. Weissman) or *D* (Dr. Dixon).

a Robots won't replace human workers because new technology will lead to new industries and jobs. _____

b People may not be comfortable with robots making decisions, especially when driving cars. _____

c Robots help doctors pay attention during long surgeries. _____

d Robots will never be able to deal with unexpected situations as well as doctors can. _____

Digging Deeper

5 Read the main ideas and complete the tables with the supporting details.

Main Idea Many things will be automated in the workplace.

Supporting Detail	Supporting Detail	Supporting Detail

Main Idea Hospitals will use robots to assist doctors during surgery.

Supporting Detail	Supporting Detail	Supporting Detail

Main Idea People are worried about using robots in too many areas.

Supporting Detail	Supporting Detail	Supporting Detail

Personalization

6 What would you do? Give reasons in each situation.

a   You need surgery. A doctor or a robot can perform the operation. Which would you choose? Why?

_____

_____

b   Your parents can drive you to school or you can take a driverless car. Which would you choose? Why?

_____

_____

c   You need a new computer. Would you choose one made by a robot or one hand-made by a human? Why?

_____

_____

_____

8 How do we know what happened in the past?

Key Words

1 🎧 **Preview the Key Words.**
8.1

| attract | armor | spread out | arch | breeze |

| vent | notice (v) | consider | silk | chopsticks |

2 **Read the definitions and write the Key Words.**

a   a soft wind _____   e   a smooth, soft material _____

b   become aware of a thing _____   f   think about something _____

c   pull a thing nearer _____   g   an opening for air _____

d   protective clothing _____   h   a curved shape _____

Pre-reading

3 **Look at the pictures on pages 115–21 and circle the things you can see.**

chopsticks   a toothbrush   footprints   brown hair

a low table   an air vent

4 **Make predictions about how these things will be important in the story.**

_____

_____

_____

5 🎧 **Listen and read.**
8.2

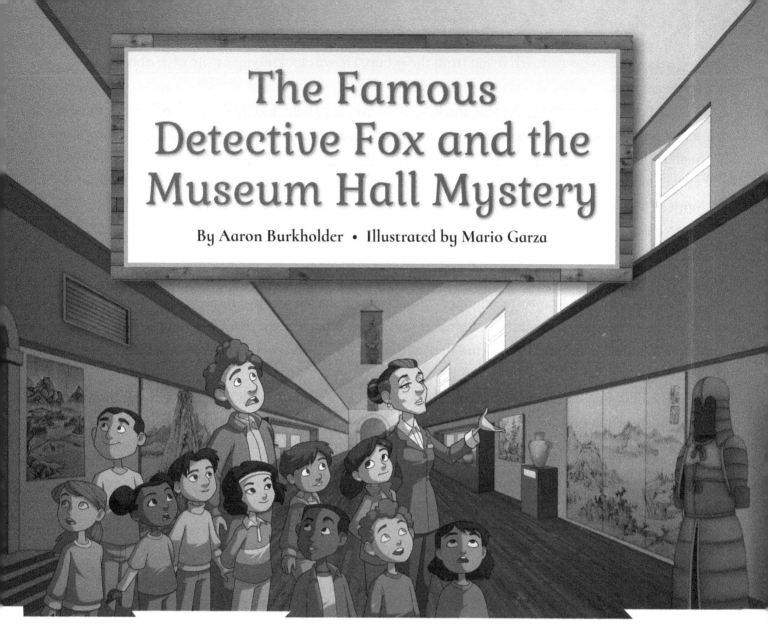

The Famous Detective Fox and the Museum Hall Mystery

By Aaron Burkholder • Illustrated by Mario Garza

"And, if you follow me into this hall, we will take a journey back to an ancient and beautiful culture. Watch your step!" Mrs. Ellis, the tour guide, announced.

"Whoa, thanks! I almost didn't see the steps down there!" said Nick. He was very tall for fifth grade.

"That's because your head is always in the clouds," said Kara. The other children laughed.

One by one, the students of Mr. Lambert's fifth grade class stepped down into the dusty old exhibition hall. It was filled with objects that were carefully arranged to attract the visitors' attention. There were pieces of vases, cups, plates, and other pottery, metal knives, part of a fresco that showed a village and mountains, a suit of armor, some old cooking and farming tools—everything looking just a little bit exotic.

The students spread out because there was too much to see all at once. "Wow, it's amazing!" said Dorothy.

"You're not kidding," replied her best friend, Nancy. She was leaning over some yellow documents, trying to make out the rivers and villages on a map.

Even Mr. Lambert walked away from the group. He was looking up at the arch above a stone column.

But Penelope Fox just stood still and looked all over the room, just as she always did. She liked to know everything about a new place or person—well, she liked to know everything about everything, really. She buttoned up her jacket and noted the breeze coming in through an air vent. She looked at the floor and counted the marks in the dust that people left there with their shoes. She also noticed Mrs. Ellis clap her hands nervously as Rob chased Lorenzo around the room.

"No running! Everyone, please, follow Mr. Lambert, and let's look at this exhibit," she called out to the class.

Rob and Lorenzo stopped just before they knocked Mr. Lambert over.

"Watch out!" Mr. Lambert exclaimed. "You almost knocked me into these people's dining room!"

The class gathered around Mr. Lambert and the two boys at the exhibit. It looked like the inside of a house. The scene was complete with a family sitting around a low table and drinking tea.

Mrs. Ellis started to explain, "An archeologist is like a detective who looks at old things and learns about the past."

"Wow, that sounds like a perfect job for you, Penelope," said Oliver. Penelope nodded.

Mrs. Ellis continued, "I'm making you all assistant archeologists for the day. Now, what do you notice about the people here?"

"They are sitting on the floor," said Emmy.

"That's right. In many countries, this is the normal way to sit at a table," said Mrs. Ellis. "Now, notice the painting on the wall and the writing, the wooden house structure, the fabric of their clothes, and—"

"And that something is missing from the exhibit!" Penelope interrupted.

"Well, there are lots of things missing from this collection, actually," said Mrs. Ellis. "It's very rare for an archeologist to find a complete set of artifacts. We have been trying to gather—"

"No, no. I mean, someone just stole something from this exhibit," Penelope replied. "In the last few minutes."

All the students gasped.

"What?"

"No way."

"A robbery!"

"Who could do that?"

Mrs. Ellis looked at the scene again. "That's not a funny joke, young lady."

"Oh! You think I'm joking. I guess you haven't noticed the father's hand then? I don't see how that's possible, but look at it now," Penelope said. They all looked at his hand.

Nick shrugged. "So, what are we supposed to see?" he asked.

Penelope looked around at the confused faces of her classmates. "You mean, you don't see it?" she asked. They shook their heads. "Look at this room. It looks like it hasn't been cleaned in days. Don't you see the dust everywhere?" They all nodded their heads. "But someone cleans this museum every day, right?" Mrs. Ellis nodded. "Well, where did all this dust come from then? Look up at that vent." Everyone turned to look at the vent and listen to it blowing in dusty air.

"We have had some trouble with the ventilation system lately," said Mrs. Ellis.

"Now, look at the father again," Penelope continued. They all looked.

"There's no dust in the middle of his hand!" Kara exclaimed, suddenly following Penelope's logic.

"Hardly any," said Penelope. "So, we know he was holding something—probably an artifact—and that it was taken in the last few minutes."

Mrs. Ellis nodded. "What you say may be true, Penelope. I think I remember he was holding something, although I can't remember what it was right now."

"Oh, no!" said Mr. Lambert, worried. "Mrs. Ellis, I'm so sorry. This is terrible."

"Well, we already know a lot about the artifact at least, so that should help us to find it," Penelope told them.

"We do?" asked Dorothy. "How? We haven't seen it."

"We don't need to see a thing to know what it looks like, do we?" asked Penelope. The rest of the students looked at each other in deeper confusion.

"We at least know it had to fit in the father's hand," she continued, "and we know what culture it was from."

"Oh! Yes, we do!" said Nancy. "Look at the painting on the wall; that's Chinese writing on it."

"That's what I thought," said Penelope, "although I can't really read it."

"Hmm, I can read Chinese, a little," said Nancy. "My parents taught me. I think it says something about a tiger and a wedding."

"That's very good!" said Mrs. Ellis. "It's from the Ming Dynasty era, over five centuries ago. Each symbol is a separate word or concept, and there are thousands of different symbols in written Chinese."

"That's right, class," said Mr. Lambert. "That's why it is so hard to learn to read and write Chinese."

"Maybe he was holding a pen!" Nancy suddenly guessed. "He might be writing Chinese!"

Mrs. Ellis considered the idea for a moment. "Yes, perhaps. Writing, poetry, and literature have been very important to the Chinese throughout their history, but they used brushes to write, not pens."

"But he wasn't holding a writing brush," Penelope added. "Just look at the table. There is no paper at his place; there's just a cup of tea."

"Maybe he was holding a fork or a spoon!" Nick guessed.

"I don't think so," said Penelope. "The family is wearing nice, bright silk robes, so they must have some money, and yet the house has no electric lights. So, this must be a scene from a long time ago."

"Uh-huh, Mrs. Ellis already told us that," replied Nick. "So, what?"

Mrs. Ellis responded, "They used chopsticks, not forks or spoons."

"Ah-ha!" said Mr. Lambert. "We should look for chopsticks then!"

"Hmm, well, not exactly, Mr. Lambert," said Penelope. "Have you ever held chopsticks? You need to hold them between your fingers and your thumb, and this man looks more like he is holding something in his fist."

"Well, that could be anything!" Oliver complained.

"Look!" Nancy suddenly shouted. "I wonder if this hair has anything to do with it."

Most of the other children, including Penelope, had to bend down to look where she was pointing, under the father's hand. When she did, Penelope exclaimed, "How silly of me."

There were a few hairs stuck to the father figure's hand.

The quiet museum became noisy with everyone talking at once.

"Where did the hair come from?"

"Maybe he had a hairbrush!"

"What did hairbrushes in ancient China look like?"

"That's it! Let's find it!"

"Everybody, look for a hairbrush!"

Mrs. Ellis tried to contain the excitement.

But before she had a chance, Penelope stepped forward, and everyone turned to her instead. "It's not a hairbrush we should be looking for," she said simply.

Everyone was about to start talking again, but Mrs. Ellis was quicker this time. "What evidence do you have?" she asked.

"Don't you see?" Penelope asked. "The hair isn't from the exhibit. It's from the thief."

Everyone looked at the brown, curly hairs under the father's hand again and then slowly turned to Mr. Lambert.

"Me?" he asked, surprised. "I didn't steal anything!"

Penelope walked around behind him. "Maybe you didn't mean to steal anything, Mr. Lambert," she said, "but don't you remember when you almost fell into this exhibit?" Rob and Lorenzo both looked around guiltily. Penelope continued, "You probably picked up the artifact then. In fact, I can see it." She reached up behind Mr. Lambert's head. "Hmm, it's a brush," she added, "but it's not supposed to be in anyone's hair."

She pulled out a small white stick of bone with boar hairs set into one end. It looked like ...

"A toothbrush?" asked Mr. Lambert.

Mrs. Ellis was smiling. "Yes," she said, "the Chinese invented the style of toothbrush that we still use today. This one is over four hundred years old."

Mr. Lambert just scratched his head and looked at the artifact again. "Well, then I'd say it's time we get him a new one."

Everyone laughed, even Mrs. Ellis. Penelope returned the artifact to Mrs. Ellis, and they all enjoyed the rest of the museum together. Penelope, of course, went on to have many more adventures as the famous Detective Fox.

Key Words

1 **Use the Key Words to solve the riddles.**

a People use these all over China.
For picking up rice, there's nothing finer.

_____

b This is another word for what you do,
When you think if something is true.

_____

c I'm super smooth and soft and shiny.
In expensive clothes is where you'll
find me.

_____

d Put this on, and you won't get hurt.
It's solid and strong like a metal shirt.

_____

e People will do this if they need some space.
They'll move apart, won't crowd up in one place.

_____

f Look up and you'll see it curving over you,
A fabulous entrance to walk right through.

_____

Comprehension

2 **Circle the correct options.**

1 What is the first exhibit?
   a a painting   b a piece of clothing   c a dining room

2 Who almost falls into the exhibit?
   a Mr. Lambert   b Mrs. Ellis   c Penelope

3 How does Mrs. Ellis react when Penelope says something is missing from the exhibit?
   a She thinks it's funny.   b She's annoyed.   c She believes her.

4 Why is the exhibit dusty?
   a Because no one cleans it.   b Because it is old.   c Because dusty air blows through the vent.

5 Who knows how to read some Chinese?
   a Nancy   b Penelope   c Mrs. Ellis

6 Why is the brush not supposed to be in anyone's hair?
   a Because it's dusty.   b Because it's made of bone.   c Because it's a toothbrush.

3 **Describe how the toothbrush got into Mr. Lambert's hair.**

_____

_____

Digging Deeper

4 Write three things Penelope notices before they look at the dining room exhibit. Why are they important?

a _____

_____

b _____

_____

c _____

_____

5 Write the deduction for each observation Penelope makes.

Observation	Deduction
There is no dust in the middle of the father's hand.	a _____ _____
There's no paper at the father's place.	b _____ _____
The father looks like he was holding something in his fist.	c _____ _____
The hair on the father's hand is curly and brown.	d _____ _____

Personalization

6 Complete the story review chart.

Story Summary: _____

_____

What I liked best: _____

_____

I didn't like: _____

I learned that: _____

It made me think about: _____

You should / shouldn't read this story because: _____

_____

Star Rating (Out of Five): _____

(8) How do we know what happened in the past?

Key Words

1 Preview the Key Words.
8.3

vivid bury snapshot graffiti prehistory

propose gorge nomadic monolith carve

2 Answer the questions.

a What types of things do people carve? _____

b Where do we often see graffiti? _____

c What kinds of colors are vivid? _____

d What kind of picture is a snapshot? _____

e What do nomadic people do? _____

f What sort of things do people propose? _____

Pre-reading

3 Look at the pictures on page 125. Predict which period of history each picture is from.

_____

_____

4 Think about how historians find out more about these periods of history. Make a list of objects and places that give them information.

_____

_____

5 Listen and read.
8.4

How History Changes

By Aaron Burkholder

What was life like for your parents when they were your age? Did they do the same things that you and your friends do? Do your parents remember the same things? What about your grandparents? We all know that many things change over time, like technology, but also words, beliefs, cities, entertainment, and much more.

But how do we find out about the past when people who lived back then aren't alive to tell us about it? Through history and the science of archeology, of course! And, each time we learn something new, it can change our picture of the past. So, let's look at some incredible historical documents and archeological discoveries and how they changed the way we understand human history.

For a long time, what we knew about Roman life came from historical documents like Pliny the Younger's *Letters*. He was a Roman politician and writer. In one vivid story, he describes being in Pompeii in 79 CE, the night Mount Vesuvius erupted:

Earthquakes were common in that part of Italy. But that night, they were very violent. My mother came into my room, and we went to sit awake and look out at the bay. By early morning, the shaking was very bad. We didn't feel safe in the streets of the city. We decided to leave. Across the bay, a huge black cloud was growing. Bright fires shot out of it. The ocean fell back and left many fish on the sand.

As we left the city, ash began to fall lightly from the sky. I looked back and saw a thick, black cloud coming toward us like a flood. "Let's get off the road while we can still see," I told my mother. "We don't want to fall down in the dark with all these people behind us." Just as we found a place to rest, everything went dark—not like a cloudy night. It was like someone put out the lamps in a closed room.

Pliny the Younger

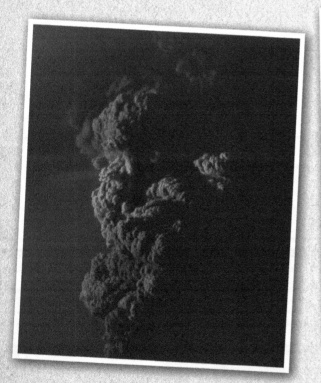

Mount Vesuvius today

The eruption killed thousands of people and buried the city in ash. Many ancient documents decay over time and, if they are not copied, are lost forever. Thankfully we have Pliny's letter to the Roman historian Tacitus. So we know something about what it was like to experience this event, which happened almost 2,000 years ago!

Except for personal letters like this one, people like Pliny the Younger mostly wrote about government, art, and famous people. They didn't tell us a lot about everyday life. For that, we can look to the archeological ruins. The destruction of Pompeii happened very quickly—in just a few hours. Ash completely covered the city. When archeologists found the ruins of the city in 1749 CE, much of it was preserved exactly as it was in 79 CE. So, the ruins are like a snapshot of a day in Roman life.

The ruins of Pompeii

For example, there were jars of fruit at the market. There were bakeries with 2,000-year-old Roman bread. And there was other evidence that shows us the Roman diet. The archeologists also found many "modern" inventions, like sliding doors, running water, a sewer, and a large hotel.

Many of Pompeii's villas were vacation spots and had beautiful frescoes. They show Roman architecture and cities, trees, gardens, and the Roman people. But, outside on the streets, there was a lot of graffiti, like in many big cities today. There was some useful graffiti, such as prices at different stores or political advertisements. There was also some less useful graffiti—things that say, for example, "Gaius was here."

By examining the ruins, preserved food, and even the graffiti, archeologists were able to get an idea of daily life for the ordinary citizens of Pompeii. In some ways, they concluded, it was similar to our lives today.

Other kinds of archeology take us even farther back in time, into prehistory. To archeologists, prehistory means the time before the invention of writing. (And history is the time period since writing.) They separate these periods because prehistoric research is different. There are no documents from these times, and there aren't "living snapshots," like the ruins of Pompeii. Instead, these archeologists look back millions of years, and the information we get comes from fossils and rocks. And locating this evidence is not easy to do.

The Olduvai Gorge

Charles Darwin proposed his theory of evolution in 1859. Many people did not believe people and apes shared a common ancestor. However, scientists immediately began looking for the ancestors of humans. But evidence was found very slowly at first.

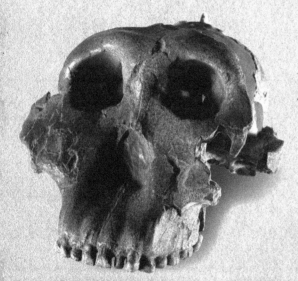

In the 1930s, for example, Mary Leakey and her husband, Louis, began excavating an area in eastern Africa called the Olduvai Gorge. They worked there for almost 50 years! During this time, they found hundreds of fossils. These were from different human ancestors that lived there at different times. They showed how humans had evolved. Even more interesting, they found many different tools at the site. Their discoveries showed that these tools evolved over millions of years.

Thanks to the Leakeys' discoveries, scientists believe civilization developed very slowly. Early humans were nomadic and had to move around a lot to hunt for food. Later, they learned how to use tools. Then, they learned how to control fire. After that, they discovered how to raise animals and plants and began to farm. Many archeologists think agriculture is the most important development in human society because people could stay in one place. That gave them time to develop cities, cultures, religion, and many new jobs.

An early stone tool

But, perhaps, that is not the whole picture after all. In 1994, German archeologist Klaus Schmidt began excavating the ruins at Göbekli Tepe, in southern Turkey. At first, it just looked like a few small stones on top of a hill. These were the tips of huge stone monoliths, large stones that people stand up vertically. Incredibly, the monoliths were dated to 10,000–8,000 BCE. Archeologists now think it is the oldest temple in the world.

But how do they know it's a temple? There are more than 200 of these monoliths in about 20 different circles at the site. Some of these monoliths are carved in different animal shapes. This suggests a religious purpose. Also, they have found no houses, cooking fires, or evidence of people living at the site. Instead, they have found the bones of thousands of animals, which suggests animals were killed for religious purposes here.

So, if Göbekli Tepe is the world's oldest temple, why is it important? It changes the way we think of prehistoric societies. We now know that early groups of nomadic people had some kind of culture. They organized and built this temple because they shared some set of beliefs. This was before humans had developed farming, the wheel, pottery, metal, or writing. So, did humans stop being nomadic before they built cities and developed culture? Or, did it happen the other way around?

We all learn about history in school. But we are always finding out more about it through the incredible discoveries made by scientists. Who knows? The next big discovery might add something new to our knowledge—and it might be made by you!

Key Words

1 **Circle the correct options to complete the sentences.**

a The bones were buried / proposed / carved deep underground.

b The cave paintings were from gorges / prehistory / monoliths. There is no written evidence from that time.

c Monoliths can be vivid / carved / buried to show animal figures.

d The gorge / monolith / graffiti was very deep, and it took an hour to hike down into it.

e Mom carved / proposed / buried going to the amusement park next weekend.

Comprehension

2 **Match the pieces of evidence to things they help us understand.**

1	Pliny the Younger's *Letters*	a	religious practices in prehistory
2	jars of fruit at the market	b	human evolution
3	graffiti	c	Mount Vesuvius's eruption
4	fossils and rocks	d	prices at the market
5	monoliths and animal bones	e	people's diet in Ancient Rome

3 **Read and circle *T* (true) or *F* (false).**

a We cannot know about life during prehistory.   T   F

b Strong earthquakes were the first evidence that Mount Vesuvius was erupting.   T   F

c The ruins of Pompeii gave a lot of information about daily Roman life.   T   F

d Pliny the Younger didn't write about important people.   T   F

e The discovery of animal bones suggested Göbekli Tepe was a temple.   T   F

f People definitely started farming before culture developed.   T   F

4 **Complete the graphic organizer.**

	What They Found	Conclusions They Made
a Archeologists in Pompeii →	→	
b Mary and Louis Leakey →	→	
c Klaus Schmidt →	→	

Digging Deeper

5 How did new evidence change the way that archeologists thought about the past?

Pompeii: _____

_____

_____

Göbekli Tepe: _____

_____

_____

6 🗨 Think of three things you didn't understand in the text. Then, write what strategies you used to clarify the meaning. Complete the chart.

	Monitor and Clarify	
I didn't understand:	**I used these strategies:**	**Now I think it means:**

Personalization

7 Think of a historical site in your country and answer the questions.

a Where is it? _____

b What was found there? _____

c When is it from? _____

d What can you learn from it? _____

8 What artifact would you leave behind so that archeologists in the future could understand your life? Explain your choice.

_____

_____

_____

Why does biodiversity matter?

Key Words

① 🎧 **Preview the Key Words.**
9.1

rugged   remedy   ailment   herb   clearing

wary   peer (v)   creep   spy   soothe

② **Read the definitions and write the Key Words.**

a a sickness or illness _____

b to look carefully or with difficulty _____

c a medicine or treatment _____

d very cautious or suspicious _____

e to move slowly and quietly _____

f to make someone feel better _____

g somewhere that is rough and rocky _____

h a plant that is used in cooking _____

Pre-reading

③ **Look at the pictures on pages 133–41. Write three questions about the story.**

a _____

b _____

c _____

④ 🎧 **Listen and read.**
9.2

Rahui and the Sierra Tarahumara

By Jenna Briggs-Fish • Illustrated by Daniela Martín del Campo

Do you have a favorite place? Mine is here on the top of this mountain. I love watching the sun light up the mountains every morning. The rugged mountains are majestic. Up here, I feel energized, but at the same time very small compared to the greatness of nature around me. This, for me, is the most awe-inspiring place on Earth.

So, where is this incredible place? Well, it's my home. I live in the Sierra Tarahumara in northern Mexico. It's an interesting mix of desert, forest, and mountain. While it can get hot here in the spring, the winter temperatures are freezing. Not many choose to live here. But my community has lived here forever. I'm part of the Rarámuri community, one of the four communities that live in these mountains. I live with my family: my mother, my father, and my two older brothers.

"Rahui!" I hear my name echo off the rocks, so I run back home.

"Where have you been?" asks my mother handing me a plate of beans. "Your grandmother's been looking for you. She has some jobs for you."

My grandmother, Bimorí, is an *owirúame*. That's what we call the healers in the Rarámuri community. I guess you'd call her a kind of doctor. She uses her knowledge of plants to heal people with natural remedies.

When I was very young, she noticed my interest in plants and began to teach me to become an *owirúame*, too. With her help, I'm learning how to make various mixtures of oils and plants to treat different ailments, like *rurawiki* (a cold) or *rorógara* (a sore throat). There's a lot to remember.

In my community, all children grow up learning the value of every living plant, and how nature needs to be respected. Up until a few months ago, I believed everyone in the world thought this way, but it turns out I was wrong.

One day, a few months ago, I was helping my grandmother. That day she had given me a list of plants to collect and sent me off into the forest. My friend Ariché decided to come along. Ariché doesn't know much about plants or medicine, but she never misses a chance to go exploring.

After a while, we had just one more herb to find—the *chuchupate*. I led Ariché deep into the forest to the place where my father had shown me where to find it, but, when we got there, we were both shocked by what we saw. Instead of a forest, there was a clearing. The beautiful tall pines that had grown there had been replaced by a pile of neatly chopped logs, and the forest floor had been turned to dust. There was no sign of the *chuchupate*. In fact, there was no sign of any plants at all.

"What's this?" I whispered. "What's going on?"

"I don't know, Rahui, but we need to find out," Ariché replied.

She took a step forward, but the sound of voices stopped her. I grabbed her hand and pulled her behind a tree. I could hear that they weren't speaking our language— it sounded like they were speaking in Spanish.

"*Chabochis,*" gasped Ariché.

"Shhh!" I hissed, trying to stop her from talking.

Chabochis is the name we give to Mexicans outside the Rarámuri community. My parents had warned me about the *Chabochis*, telling me stories of how they want to steal what is rightfully ours and destroy our traditions. Most of the time, they have no reason to be on our land, so to hear their language so close made me wary. Who were they? What were they doing?

"We have to get a better look," said Ariché.

"You can't go in there. What if someone sees you?" I said. "We'll come back later when it's dark. Right now, we better get back."

There was a party planned for that evening in our community. So, while our families were busy with the celebration and ritual dance, Ariché and I snuck back to the forest without anyone seeing us.

Back at the edge of the clearing, protected by the darkness, we peered through the pine trees. All was quiet.

"I'm going in. Are you coming?" whispered Ariché as she crept through the trees.

She didn't wait for my answer, so I followed her. I saw her pause near the pile of logs we had seen that morning. She placed the palm of her hand against the smooth end of one of the logs. I could see she was upset. We both were. There were easily twenty trees piled up.

I turned around, and what I saw made me even more afraid.

"Ariché," I said slowly. "You need to see this."

Instead of twenty logs, there were hundreds. We walked out further into the clearing and realized the damage was much greater than we had imagined. The logs lay everywhere, some on the ground, others already loaded onto trucks. We stared at the devastation with our mouths wide open.

"They're coming in the morning to take the first batch," called a voice in Spanish.

The men were still here, and we were standing alone in the middle of the clearing. We heard a truck door slam shut. We turned to run back to the trees behind us, but a large man blocked our path.

"What do we have here?" The words came from the man. "A little pair of spies. Do you know what we do with spies around here?"

We heard the sound of a chainsaw, and the man laughed at our fear.

Ariché and I had the same instinctive reaction. We ran. We ran and didn't look back. We could hear the shouts from the men behind but kept on running faster than we've ever run before. We didn't stop until we reached home. Our mothers were furious that we had missed the party, but we were just relieved to be back.

The next two days I was quieter than usual, and I tried to distract myself with my usual tasks. It was working until my grandmother asked me again for some *chuchupate*. She said she needed it to treat my brother, Suré.

"What's wrong with him?" I asked.

"His throat infection has gotten worse, but I'm sure my *chuchupate* mixture will soothe him. Do you have any?"

The truth was that I hadn't gone back to the clearing. The incident with the loggers had terrified me. They were dangerous, and it seemed they wouldn't let anything stop them. And yet, something had to be done before they destroyed more of the forest and wiped out more valuable plants.

My grandmother noticed my hesitation. It was impossible to hide anything from her.

"I could give him something else, but it wouldn't work as well as the *chuchupate*. Now run and get it, Rahui!"

"I can't," I admitted.

I was forced to tell her everything—about the clearing, the logs, the men.

That afternoon, a community
meeting was called. Soon everyone knew
about what had happened. My father spoke
to the group and reminded everyone that this
was not the first time the *Chabochis* had done this. He
explained that, for many years, the *Chabochis* had cut
down trees on our land. When he warned everyone to stay
away from the clearing, he looked directly at Ariché and me.
He was upset that we had gotten involved in this.

"But, Father," I said, "they've taken all the *chuchupate*. They're
clearing the only area where it grows, and Grandmother Bimorí
needs it to heal Suré."

"Is he right?" said a female voice from the crowd. "Surely not. Our lands are huge,
and it must grow elsewhere."

"The boy is right," Grandmother Bimorí spoke up. "We have searched everywhere,
but that is the only place we have found where the soil is right and the *chuchupate*
grows well every year. I understand your concern Rahui. The plant is important,
but you are more important. We have to stay away."

"Rahui, what are we going to do?" Ariché asked me later when we were alone.

"I don't know, Ariché, but we've seen that we need something or someone more powerful than us
to stop them." I thought and thought. "Wait a minute. Don't you have a cousin at the University
of Chihuahua? You once told me he was involved in ecology, didn't you?"

"Andrés? He's just a student.
I'm not sure how he can help us."

"Neither am I, but he's our best hope.
When is your mother going to the city to sell crafts?"

"Tomorrow."

"Great. That's my chance."

The next morning, I accompanied the women and girls on the long, uncomfortable journey to Chihuahua. My father had agreed to let me go because he thought it would be better if I was farther away from the men in the clearing. On the way, I asked Ariché's mother about her nephew Andrés and the university. She was proud to talk about her nephew and didn't suspect anything when I asked her for directions.

When it was time to get down from the truck, the women unloaded the handwoven baskets and pots, and I snuck away, and started running in the direction of the university.

At the entrance, I saw Andrés walking toward me. He looked more like a *Chabochi* in his jeans and shirt, but he greeted me like a true Rarámuri. He took me to the cafeteria, and I explained to him what was going on in the mountains. He was shocked and saddened, but his words gave me hope. He said he would see what he could do.

Yesterday, Andrés visited us in the sierra. He had some good news. He told our story to a group called *Tarahumara Forever*, which works to protect the Sierra Tarahumara, and they agreed to help. He told us not to worry because the loggers wouldn't be back.

I wasn't sure if I believed him, so I decided to return to the clearing. Once again, I heard voices. I was about to turn and run, but I didn't because I saw something in the clearing—something that made me smile. Instead of machines, or chainsaws, or piles of logs, I saw people—lots of *Chabochis*, planting trees. Andrés had been right—maybe not all *Chabochis* were bad after all. Some did care.

As I started the long walk back home, something else caught my eye. It looked familiar. Looking closer, I saw a lonely *chuchupate* shoot! It had survived the invasion after all.

Key Words

1 Complete the sentences with the correct form of the Key Words.

| rugged | wary | herb | clearing | spy | soothe | creep |

a We picked _____ from the garden to make this medicinal tea.

b You need a lot of strength to climb those _____ mountains.

c I drank some hot tea to _____ my sore throat.

d There was a _____ in the center of the forest where they planned to build a hotel.

e They _____ around the forest so that the men won't hear or see them.

f He tried to listen to what we were saying and see what we were doing. I think he might have been a _____.

g We were _____ of the dog because it seemed like it would bite.

Comprehension

2 Circle the correct option.

1 What is the weather like in the sierra?

  a always hot   b always cold   c hot and cold

2 What did Rahui and Ariché find in the clearing at the beginning of the story?

  a tall pine trees   b stacked logs   c *chuchupate*

3 How do they feel when they see the trucks?

  a shocked and upset   b angry   c scared

4 Rahui doesn't want to go back to the clearing because he is scared of …

  a the loggers.   b his mother.   c his grandmother.

5 Why does Rahui go to Chihuahua?

  a to sell crafts   b to find *chuchupate*   c to talk to Ariché's cousin

6 What doesn't Rahui see at the end of the story?

  a people planting trees   b a *chuchupate* shoot   c machines

3 Answer the questions.

a What did Rahui's parents say that the *Chabochis* wanted to do?

_____

b What was decided at the community meeting?

_____

c What does Rahui realize about the *Chabochis* at the end of the story?

_____

Digging Deeper

4 Read the lines from the story and write notes about what the words in bold mean.

a The rugged mountains are **majestic**. _____

_____

b Ariché and I had the same **instinctive** reaction. _____

_____

c Our mothers were **furious** that we had missed the party. _____

_____

5 Reread the sentences in Activity 4. Then, close your eyes and visualize each sentence. **What do you see?**

a _____

b _____

c _____

6 Read the story again. Choose three difficult words and guess what they mean.

I didn't understand:	Now I think it means:
a _____	_____
b _____	_____
c _____	_____

7 Complete the table with the plot's main problem and the resolution

Problem	Resolution
_____	_____
_____	_____
_____	_____

Personalization

8 Think of an environmental problem in your community (e.g., traffic, deforestation, not enough water). Then, answer the questions.

a What is the problem?

_____

b What is the cause of the problem?

_____

c What can people do about it?

_____

9 Why does biodiversity matter?

Key Words

1 **Preview the Key Words.**
9.3

shoreline   high tide   low tide   bay   bulge (v)

align   intertidal zone   tide pool   seaweed   sea urchin

2 **Read the definitions and write the Key Words.**

a   part of a large body of water that is surrounded by land _____

b   a creature that has a lot of colorful spikes _____

c   the land along the edge of a body of water _____

d   to look larger or rounder than normal _____

e   to arrange things so that they form a line _____

f   a type of plant that grows in the ocean _____

Pre-reading

3 **Read the title and look at the pictures on pages 145–49. Write three things you know about tides.**

a   _____

b   _____

c   _____

4 **Write three things you would like to learn about tides.**

a   _____

b   _____

c   _____

5 **Listen and read.**
9.4

The Secrets of the Tides

By Kellie Dundon

How Do Tides Work?

When you're at the beach, it can be fascinating to watch the waves roll in toward the shore. They rush up the sand and then sweep back out to the ocean. Waves do this over and over again, all day and all night.

The farthest point that waves stretch up to on the beach is called the shoreline, and the shoreline can change a lot throughout the day. That's because the strength of the waves and the distance they travel depends on the time of day. Two times each day, the waves are higher and come the farthest inshore. This is known as high tide. Two times each day, it's the opposite, and the waves come the least far inshore. This is known as low tide.

At some beaches, the difference between high tide and low tide is much more noticeable than it is at others. Beaches that are long and straight see less of a tide range, since the high tide water spreads over a bigger area. In protected, narrow bays, the water is closed into a smaller area. So the big swells of water at high tide and shallower water at low tide are very different, and we see a much more noticeable tide range.

Did You Know?

- There are 620,000 kilometers of coastline on Earth.

- About 71% of Earth's surface is water.

- The moon causes high and low tides.

What Causes Tides?

At nighttime, and sometimes even during the day, we see the moon up in the sky. It looks like it's a long way away, and it is! But it affects things happening right here on Earth, such as the tide. The moon exerts a gravitational pull on Earth causing the water to lift up or bulge on the side of Earth closest to the moon. The same thing happens on the side of Earth farthest from the moon.

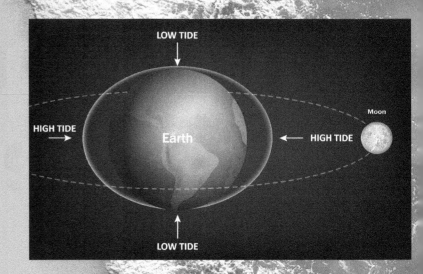

Because Earth rotates constantly, the part of Earth that is passing through one of these two bulges is always changing. When a beach passes through one of these bulges, it has a high tide. Every time a beach passes the area between the bulges, it experiences a low tide. This cycle repeats twice each day, at slightly different times because the moon also revolves around Earth.

During a full moon or new moon, the sun, the moon, and Earth align. The gravitational pull of the sun and the moon combine and create more extreme tides. This is why, every two weeks, there are very high tides known as spring tides and very low tides known as neap tides.

And, have you ever heard of a king tide? That's the biggest tide of all! It's caused when both the moon and the sun are really close to Earth at the same time. King tides happen once or twice every year. They are normal and totally predictable events.

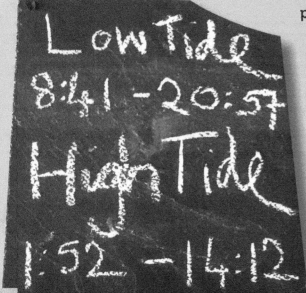

Having Fun with Tides

People who surf or fish at the beach often check the local newspaper or online to see what time of day high and low tide will be. It will depend on the conditions at your own beach, but a lot of surfers prefer to go surfing at high tide, when the waves are the biggest. And a lot of fishermen think fishing is the best between high and low tide, when there is more movement in the water.

The cycle of high and low tides is also very important for the plants and animals that live in the intertidal zone. This zone is the area that is underwater at high tide and above water at low tide. Waves fill the hollow rock areas or big sandy holes on the beach with fascinating sea life, and, when the tide goes out, you can explore the rich biodiversity of these tide pools.

The next time you go to the beach, look closely at the tide pools. You might be surprised by what you see! Here are just some of the plants and animals you could find in a tide pool: crabs, octopuses, anemones, and starfish. Look for small fish, sea snails, seaweed, and algae. See if you can spot seahorses, clams, or mussels. Check for sea urchins, sea cucumbers, and more!

There's lots of fun to be had with waves. Have you ever tried these activities?

- boogie-boarding, bodysurfing, or paddle-boarding
- fishing
- skim-boarding or jumping over waves

Amazing Tide Pools

Did you know that starfish can regrow their arms if they get cut off? Or that crabs not only walk sideways but also swim sideways? Or that an octopus has three hearts and that its blood is colored blue? These are just some of the amazing things you can learn about the creatures that live in tide pools.

Starfish

And the plants you can find in tide pools are pretty cool, too. Seaweed, for example, is a plant, but it doesn't have roots, stems, leaves, or flowers. Instead, it has something called a "holdfast" that connects it to rocks and blades that look and act a lot like leaves. Some seaweeds even have parts that are filled with gas to help the blades float near the surface of the water. Floating near the water's surface allows the blades to be exposed to sunlight and to carry out photosynthesis. And, many seaweeds are very healthy foods, but don't eat any seaweed you find in a tide pool.

Seaweed

In fact, you should never disturb the animal or plant life you find in tide pools. It's safer for the sea life and for you, too, if you don't touch anything. The creatures you see can easily be eaten by predators like seagulls when it is low tide. So, over time, they have developed ways to defend themselves from danger. Crabs can pinch with their claws. The spines of sea urchins are sharp and spiky. And there are some creatures—like the blue-ringed octopus— that protect themselves with venom. Their venom is poisonous to humans, too!

Take a Close Look

Tide pool creatures also protect themselves from predators by hiding or using camouflage. Seahorses take on the color and shape of their habitat so that they're hard to see. Octopuses can change color to match their surroundings and to blend in. They not only do that to hide from predators, but also to help them sneak up on their prey. Sea urchins don't camouflage by changing color; they use a different trick. They cover themselves in whatever they can find. Then, there's the carrier crab, which uses its back legs to carry an urchin on its back. So when you're looking for life in a tide pool, you'll need to look really carefully if you want to see one of these tricky camouflaged creatures!

Can you spot the octopus?

Be a Beach Hero!

After a big day exploring tide pools, it's time to go home. And, of course, you should take your trash with you. The beach is a wonderful, natural place for us to enjoy, and it's our job to keep it clean for the creatures that live there.

You might even be a beach hero. To be a beach hero, take a bag with you to pick up any extra trash you see while you're exploring. That way, you'll leave the beach even cleaner than you found it. And you'll be protecting the amazing biodiversity of the tide pools!

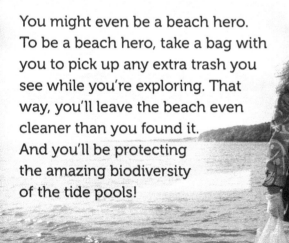

Let's Go to the Beach!

Here's what you'll need to pack for a day at the beach:

- a magnifying glass, for exploring tide pools

- a hat, sunglasses, and sunscreen to be sun-smart

- a bathing suit and a towel to swim in the ocean after a day of tide-pooling

- a notebook to write down what you discover

- a book to learn about the plants and animals you find

149

Key Words

1 **Write what the examples from the text refer to.**

| high tide | low tide | tide pool | intertidal zone | seaweed | bay |

a "The waves come the least far inshore." _____.

b "This zone is the area that is underwater at high tide and above water at low tide." _____.

c "Waves fill the hollow rock areas or big sandy holes on the beach with fascinating sea life." _____.

d "The waves are higher and come the farthest inshore." _____.

e "The water is closed into a smaller area." _____.

f "It doesn't have roots, stems, leaves, or flowers." _____.

Comprehension

2 **Read and circle T (true) or F (false).**

a The shoreline stays the same throughout the day.   T   F

b High tide happens because the moon pulls at water on the   T   F
Earth's surface.

c High tide and low tide each happen once a day.   T   F

d You can explore tide pools at high tide.   T   F

e Claws, spines, and venom are forms of defense.   T   F

f You need a bathing suit and towel to go tide-pooling.   T   F

3 **Complete the spidergrams. Add examples from the text.**

crabs

fishing

Marine
Life

Beach
Activities

Digging Deeper

4 📖 **Read the paraphrases and underline the original sentences in the text.**

a The reason for this is that how strong waves are and how far they travel depends on what time it is. (p. 145)

b It seems to be far away, and that's true! (p. 146)

c And many fishermen prefer to fish when it is neither high nor low tide because the water is moving around more. (p. 147)

d Blades that float near the top of the water get sunlight, which helps them to photosynthesize. (p. 148)

e Octopuses camouflage themselves by changing to the same color as their environment. (p. 149)

5 ✏️ **Underline the important information in the sentences. Then, paraphrase them in your own words.**

a Beaches that are long and straight see less of a tide range, since the high tide water spreads over a bigger area.

_____

_____

b At nighttime, and sometimes even during the day, we see the moon up in the sky.

_____

_____

c People who surf or fish at the beach often check the local newspaper or online to see what time of day high and low tide will be.

_____

_____

d In fact, you should never disturb the animal or plant life you find in tide pools.

_____

_____

e They not only do that to hide from predators, but also to help them sneak up on their prey.

_____

_____

Personalization

6 **What is the most interesting thing you learned from the article?**

_____

_____

Acknowledgments

The authors and publishers acknowledge the following sources of copyright material and are grateful for the permissions granted. While every effort has been made, it has not always been possible to identify the sources of all the material used or to trace all copyright holders. If any omissions are brought to our notice, we will be happy to include the appropriate acknowledgments on reprinting and in the next update to the digital edition, as applicable.

Key: U = Unit.

Photographs

All the photos are sourced from Getty Images.

U1: Allkindza/E+; photka/iStock/Getty Images Plus; imran kadir photography/Moment; SrdjanPav/E+; vgajic/E+; Grant Faint/The Image Bank; Angela26/iStock/Getty Images Plus; dickcraft/iStock/Getty Images Plus; Erik Isakson; Simon Ritzmann/Photodisc; Faysal Ahamed/iStock/Getty Images Plus; Kelly Redinger; mikroman6/Moment; AndreyPopov/iStock/Getty Images Plus; LockieCurrie/E+; Giuseppe Manfra/Moment; Xuanyu Han/Moment; REB Images/Image Source; solarseven/iStock/Getty Images Plus; Ben Stansall/AFP; Filippo Monteforte/AFP; Finnbarr Webster/Getty Images News; Fabrice Coffrini/AFP; Andrew Merry/Moment; Sirachai Arunrugstichai/Moment; ekvals/E+; NurPhoto;

U2: Westend61; tanda_V/iStock/Getty Images Plus; Jared Eygabroad/EyeEm; Chee Siong Teh/EyeEm; rozdemir01/iStock/Getty Images Plus; Fancy/Veer/Corbis; Creative Photographer specialising in Liquid/Moment; Rob Lewine; Fuse/Corbis; Jupiterimages/PHOTOS.com/Getty Images Plus; Adam Gault/OJO Images; Peter Zelei Images/Moment; SDI Productions/E+; Plattform; Halfpoint/iStock/Getty Images Plus; photosindia; vasiliki/E+; Henn Photography/Cultura; Robert Daly/OJO Images; Regis Lagrange/EyeEm; katleho Seisa/E+; ajkkafe/iStock/Getty Images Plus; Visions of America/UIG/Publisher Mix; Science Photo Library; kickstand/E+; Marion Post Wolcott/Archive Photos; clearstockconcepts/iStock/Getty Images Plus; Mccallk69/iStock Editorial; Coast-to-Coast/iStock Editorial; Margarita Sonnenberg/EyeEm; DenisTangneyJr/iStock Unreleased; AWL Images; petekarici/iStock/Getty Images Plus; FatCamera/E+; **U3:** Andrey Pozharskiy/Moment; Marco Bottigelli/Moment; MarianVejcik/iStock/Getty Images Plus; Daniel Grill; Jose Luis Pelaez Inc/DigitalVision; Imgorthand/E+; Paffy69/iStock/Getty Images Plus; susan.k./Moment; themacx/iStock/Getty Images Plus; Nutkamol Komolvanich/Moment; MathieuRivrin/Moment; Frank Smout Images/Fototrove; RichLegg/iStock/Getty Images Plus; Natasha Brown/EyeEm/EyeEm Premium; Maxiphoto/iStock/Getty Images Plus; Jim Cornfield/The Image Bank Unreleased; Jobalou/DigitalVision Vectors; Tom Chance; joakimbkk/E+; Chip Simons/Stockbyte; Westend61; Michael H Spivak/Moment; Sjo/E+; mscornelius/iStock/Getty Images Plus; John Lund/Stone; Keystone-France/Gamma-Keystone; Germán Vogel/Moment; PhotoQuest/Archive Photos; john finney photography/Moment; FrankRamspott/E+; VectorMine/iStock/Getty Images Plus; b44022101/iStock/Getty Images Plus; Rainer Lesniewski/iStock/Getty Images Plus; **U4:** fotostorm/iStock/Getty Images Plus; Rubberball/Mark Andersen; imtmphoto/iStock/Getty Images Plus; Nathan Blaney/Photodisc; Igor-Kardasov/iStock/Getty Images Plus; Alex Belomlinsky/DigitalVision Vectors; Reinhard Krull/EyeEm; Sadeugra/E+; kali9/E+; Yuri_Arcurs/E+; SensorSpot/E+; Comstock Images/Stockbyte; freemixer/E+; zelyanodzevo/iStock/Getty Images Plus; Don Farrall/Photodisc; Thomas Barwick/DigitalVision; Manisha Pandit/Moment; Victoria Gnatiuk/iStock/Getty Images Plus; Shoji Fujita/DigitalVision; LightFieldStudios/iStock/Getty Images Plus; David Sacks/The Image Bank; Koldunov/iStock/Getty Images Plus; Guylain Doyle/Lonely Planet Images; avdeev007/iStock/Getty Images Plus; DenKuvaiev/iStock Editorial; Silver Screen Collection/Moviepix; Lisa Maree Williams/Getty Images Entertainment; JGI/Jamie Grill; f9photos/iStock/Getty Images Plus; Hulton Archive; SteveStone/iStock/Getty Images Plus; AaronAmat/iStock/Getty Images Plus; SIphotography/iStock/Getty Images Plus; **U5:** John Block/The Image Bank; Fuse/Corbis; Steffen Egly/Moment Open; Thinkstock/Stockbyte; Calamity_John/iStock/Getty Images Plus; MarcelaC/iStock/Getty Images Plus; dossyl/iStock/Getty Images Plus; CiydemImages/iStock/Getty Images Plus; aaaaimages/Moment; jamesbenet/E+; Cavan Images; Bulat Silvia/iStock/Getty Images Plus; Chris_Paris/iStock/Getty Images Plus; Mike Svoboda/DigitalVision; SW Productions./Photodisc; LeventKonuk/iStock/Getty Images Plus; Steven Puetzer/Photographer's Choice RF; Morsa Images/DigitalVision; Inti St Clair/DigitalVision; SolStock/E+; SDI Productions/iStock/Getty Images Plus; Layla Dartry/EyeEm; tap10/iStock/Getty Images Plus; PeopleImages/E+; imtmphoto/iStock/Getty Images Plus; Tetra Images; vgajic/E+; Juanmonino/E+; KMM Productions/Cultura; SDI Productions/E+; Adriana Varela Photography/Moment Open; South_agency/E+; Suphansa Subruaɣɣing/iStock/Getty Images Plus; India Picture; AzmanL/iStock/Getty Images Plus; PeopleImages/iStock/Getty Images Plus; cynoclub/iStock/Getty Images Plus; Frank Smout Images/Stone; **U6:** Image Source; Jrleyland/iStock/Getty Images Plus; Colby Lysne/iStock/Getty Images Plus; Vicki Brown/Moment Open; Vester Martin/500px; Stéphane Moser/EyeEm; Monkey Business Images; MirageC/Moment; BrianAJackson/iStock/Getty Images Plus; PeopleImages/E+; Andersen Ross/DigitalVision; Science Photo Library; Cherkas/iStock/Getty Images Plus; rbmiles/iStock/Getty Images Plus; mikdam/iStock/Getty Images Plus; Matthieu Spohn/PhotoAlto Agency RF Collections; John Lund/DigitalVision; Jorg Greuel/DigitalVision; laindiapiaroa; akinbostanci/E+; benedek/iStock Unreleased; AntonioSalaverry/iStock/Getty Images Plus; Photos.com; Print Collector/Hulton Archive; Matt Carey/Moment; Alistair Berg/DigitalVision; MarkPapas/E+; ParkerDeen/E+; MediaProduction/E+; Aaron Morris/Moment; **U7:** leezsnow/E+; VladK213/iStock/Getty Images Plus; Fuse/Corbis; mbbirdy/E+; Sharon Mccutcheon/EyeEm; justme_yo/iStock/Getty Images Plus; Antagain/E+; Luisrftc/iStock/Getty Images Plus; Sompong Rattanakunchon/Moment; posteriori/E+; Sean Gladwell/Moment; Mint Images/Mint Images RF; d3sign/Moment; Morsa Images/DigitalVision; Jose Luis Pelaez Inc/DigitalVision; Perboge/iStock/Getty Images Plus; Construction Photography/Avalon/Hulton Archive; fizkes/iStock/Getty Images Plus; Tashi-Delek/E+; Erich Auerbach/Hulton Archive; esp2k/iStock/Getty Images Plus; Monty Rakusen/Cultura; zoranm/E+; Michael Chapman/iStock Editorial; darekm101/RooM; JazzIRT/E+; 3alexd/iStock/Getty Images Plus; gorodenkoff/iStock/Getty Images Plus; R_Type/iStock/Getty Images Plus; Peter Cade/Stone; Artur Kolomiyets/EyeEm; **U8:** themoog/E+; Dirk Lampersbach/EyeEm; Vladimir Serov; Vladimir Godnik; luchschen/iStock/Getty Images Plus; Klaus Vedfelt/DigitalVision; Sirikorn Thamniyom/EyeEm; PeopleImages/E+; Vyacheslav Argenberg/Moment; Chee Siong Teh/EyeEm; portishead1/E+; PM Images/Stone; Alexander Spatari/Moment; urbazon/E+; Sumiko Scott/Moment; DAJ; Ramiro Torrents/Moment; SeppFriedhuber/iStock Unreleased; David Clapp/Stone; Luis Diaz Devesa/Moment Open; Blend Images - JGI/Jamie Grill; skilpad/E+; LorenzoT81/iStock/Getty Images Plus; Tetra Images; ilbusca/iStock/Getty Images Plus; H. Armstrong Roberts/Retrofile RF; jerrytanigue/RooM; Bettmann; Andrey Nyrkov/EyeEm; Dhwee/Moment; Paolo Cordoni/EyeEm; MartinM303/iStock/Getty Images Plus; nata_rass/iStock/Getty Images Plus; Fernando Fernandes/EyeEm; Jeff Foott/Photodisc; znm/iStock/Getty Images Plus; microgen/iStock/Getty Images Plus; DEA/A. DAGLI ORTI/De Agostini; jgaunion/iStock/Getty Images Plus; xefstock/iStock/Getty Images Plus; uchar/iStock/Getty Images Plus; asikkk/iStock/Getty Images Plus; Marta Ortiz/iStock/Getty Images Plus; negatina/Moment; Ulrike Schmitt-Hartmann/DigitalVision; Tara Moore/DigitalVision; Robert Alford/iStock/Getty Images Plus; **U9:** Steve Deakin/500px; Jose Luis Pelaez Inc/DigitalVision; The Image Bank; Westend61; Mark Gerum; Leland Bobbe/Photodisc; DEMIURGE_100/iStock/Getty Images Plus; riskms/iStock/Getty Images Plus; RichVintage/E+; kali9/E+; Nearmap/DigitalVision; R A Kearton/Moment; Feifei Cui-Paoluzzo/Moment; Martin Barraud/OJO Images; magnetcreative/E+; Tracey Heong/EyeEm; Douglas Klug/Moment; Kathi Moore/EyeEm; Ed Reschke/Stone; Yinwei Liu/Moment; Nicholas Hall; Marilyn Root/Photodisc; Sollina Images; Kelly Mooney/500Px Plus; Dave Porter Peterborough Uk/Photographer's Choice; Bonnie McCann/iStock/Getty Images Plus; jf/Cultura; Yew! Images/Image Source.

Illustrations

Axel Rangel; Daniela Martín del Campo; Emmanuel Urueta; Flor Aguilar; Israel Ramírez; Marco Antonio Reyes; Mario Garza; Ricardo Figueroa; Sheila Cabeza de Vaca.

Cover artwork commissioned by Aphik S.A. de C.V

Cover illustration by Israel Ramírez

Page make-up

Aphik S.A. de C.V.